MUSICIAN'S YOGA

A Guide to Practice, Performance, and Inspiration

Mia Olson
Edited by Jonathan Feist

Berklee Press

Vice President: David Kusek
Dean of Continuing Education: Debbie Cavalier
Chief Operating Officer: Robert F. Green
Managing Editor: Jonathan Feist
Editorial Assistants: Emily Goldstein, Rajasri Mallikarjuna
Contributing Editor: Richard Mattulina
Cover Designer/Illustrator: June Olson

ISBN: 978-0-87639-095-5

1140 Boylston Street
Boston, MA 02215-3693 USA
(617) 747-2146

Visit Berklee Press Online at
www.berkleepress.com

DISTRIBUTED BY

HAL•LEONARD®
CORPORATION
7777 W. BLUEMOUND RD. P.O. BOX 13819
MILWAUKEE, WISCONSIN 53213

Visit Hal Leonard Online at
www.halleonard.com

CONTENTS

ACKNOWLEDGMENTS

There have been so many people that have helped in the making of this book.

I would first like to thank the many music and yoga teachers that I have had over the years. The love of what you all do has been an inspiration for me on my journey. I am honored to pass along the yoga tradition to the music world.

Secondly, I would like to thank the Berklee community for believing in the value and importance of these *Musician's Yoga* classes that I have developed. Throughout the years I have been able to share with so many students, faculty, and staff from around the world. Without the support of this community and all of my students, this book would not have been possible.

Thank you to Jonathan Feist, Debbie Cavalier, and all of the people at Berklee Press and Hal Leonard for making this book become a reality. I appreciate all of your efforts.

Many thanks to Fred Bouchard, Eddie Gomez, Guruatma Sing Khalsa, Barbara LaFitte, Matt Marvuglio, and Danilo Perez. I appreciate your friendship and support.

Thanks to Javier Flores-Mavil and Gema Muñoz (my chimonga). Javier was the first musical director to have me share my *Musician's Yoga* classes internationally with his *Seminario Internacional de Jazz* in Mexico. Thank you also to the many other directors.

I have much gratitude for the friendship and support of my dear friends Ted and Evie Michon. Thank you Evie for planting the writing seed in my head years ago and nudging me along the way. I finally did it!

I am grateful for the friendship of Gail and Richard Mattulina. Thank you *so* much Richard for your editing contributions. And Gail, don't worry when Richard starts waving his hands. He is just practicing his newfound techniques!

Thank you to my parents, Darold and June, and to my brother Eric, who have been an incredible source of ongoing support. A special thanks goes out to my mother for doing all of the graphics. It is wonderful to have you be an important part of this project.

There are not enough ways that I can possibly say thank you to Matt. You have contributed to the creation of this book on so many levels. Thanks for your encouragement, wisdom, ideas, and humor.

INTRODUCTION

When we practice yoga, we practice awareness. We practice awareness of our breath, posture, body, and mind. When we practice our instrument, we should also be practicing these same techniques, but usually don't. We spend more time focusing on getting the right notes and rhythms. By integrating music with yoga into our daily practice routines, we will learn how to bring awareness to how we practice and hold our instrument, so that we can learn to play with ease, calm the nerves, and let go of distracting mind chatter in order to enhance our performance.

There are also many additional benefits to practicing yoga exercises regularly. They include, but are not limited to, increasing your energy and flexibility, strengthening and toning your body, releasing tension and stress, and improving balance and concentration. Yoga helps center and ground your whole being for whatever task is at hand in your daily living.

The techniques that I will be sharing with you are applicable to all musicians, whether at a professional or a novice level. They are applicable to any instrumentalist or vocalist, or any performance situation or style of music.

We will learn the necessary yoga tools and exercises to develop a focused and concentrated mind for performance, and an awareness of the body to allow for proper posture and ease of movement, strengthening the mind-body connection. Integrating yoga into your practice routines will help you to develop an overall awareness of your body. It will help you prevent overuse injuries and help heal injuries that are already present. It will also provide an overall awareness of breath to help with musical phrasing, sound production, relaxation, and being centered and focused while performing.

Whether you are a seasoned professional musician, just starting your music career, a college student, or just starting to learn your instrument, you can benefit from practicing these simple exercises and techniques.

The book is organized so that you can move from chapter to chapter to address your specific needs. We will talk about how to practice yoga with music for performance. We will talk about breathing, meditation, posture and alignment, exercises for upper and lower body, exercises for balance, focus and concentration. We will discuss ways to take care of yourself, and ways to develop your own practice routine. You don't necessarily have to read each chapter in sequence. You can try individual exercises and then take the ones that work well for you and create your own sequence.

Practice routines appear at the end of each chapter for the specific areas of the body. There are also sample practice routines in "Developing Your Own Practice Routine" (chapter 10). All musicians should pay careful attention to the first part of "Breathing Techniques" (chapter 2) and how to do the **full yogic breath**. If you have any specific areas of the body that you would like to focus on right away, you can go to that particular chapter and learn those exercises first.

All of the stories that I will be sharing with you either come from experiences that I have had, that my students have had, or that other musicians have shared with me. The quotes come from my students. They describe how practicing yoga techniques with music have helped them. I talk about the techniques or postures that I will be covering, and then give you full details on how to do those techniques or postures. Afterward, I include a detailed practice routine, "Put It into Practice," for you to follow for that particular technique or area of the body with specific points to keep in mind.

At the end of each chapter is a chart for easy reference to the benefits of each technique or posture. So, once you learn the various techniques and poses, you will be able choose what you want to do or need for a particular day. When you are learning a new technique or exercise, it may be helpful for you to have someone read the instructions to you. You could also record yourself reading the instructions and listen to the recording. There is something very powerful about listening to your own voice instructing you in what to do.

The yoga exercises in this book are the ones that I have found most beneficial for musicians and that are easy to practice almost anywhere. There are many different styles of yoga, but since my training and practice has been mostly in the Kripalu and Kundalini traditions, most of the exercises have come from these styles. You will not need a yoga mat, but you may be more comfortable practicing with one for some of the exercises. If you would like to continue learning more yoga postures—which I would encourage—I list several books and Web sites in the Resources appendix.

    🧘 I will be using this icon throughout the book as a way to identify the beginning and the end of the various exercises that you should practice. This way, you will know when to do the exercises and when to read.

KNOW YOUR LIMITS

In doing any physical exercise, it is important to consult with your doctor as to what is appropriate for you. Do not do anything that causes a sharp pain. If you feel a sharp pain while doing any of the exercises, back away immediately. It is a sign that your body is in danger. The exercises should never be painful. If you feel pain, the exercise may not be appropriate for you in that particular moment, or you may be forcing too much. We are trying to develop a mind-body connection and honor what we discover. It is not at all about what you *think* you should be able to do. Injuries happen when the mind gets in the way of what the body is trying to tell us, or when we simply don't listen to what the body is saying.

You may feel some strain or muscle fatigue; this is what happens when you stretch and strengthen the muscles. It is normal, but it should never be a sharp sensation.

A good rule of thumb is to make sure that you always listen to your body and your breath. While practicing yoga, the breath is an indication as to how far you should stretch. If you are holding your breath, this is usually a sign that you are doing something that is too difficult, and you should back away, or you may have just lost your focus on the breath. If this happens, acknowledge it without judgment, and connect back with your full, deep breath. Find a challenging stretch in which you can keep the breath flowing freely the whole time.

Work closely with the breath in each of the stretches and exercises. Use the in breath to back away slightly from the stretch, and use the out breath to deepen the stretch. Inhale, back away from your edge. Exhale, come closer to your new edge—that point where you can feel a stretch and the muscles working but there is no sharp sensation or pain. By using the breath in this way, you can deepen the stretch gradually and safely. Making these micro movements will help deepen the stretches. You will see your edge change and move further away as you breathe into the stretch. Rather than going to your limit right away and holding the stretch and the breath, allow the breath to be your guide. Move with the breath.

Never go past your limits. This cannot be overstated. In the beginning, you may not know what your limits are, so it is important to move into each one of the postures and stretches slowly and gradually. As you develop a mind-body connection, by always moving slowly into and out of a stretch or posture, working with the breath, you will begin to develop this awareness. Sometimes you feel like you have a lot of energy, and other times you don't. It is important to stay in the present moment when you practice. Some of the things you did yesterday may not be appropriate for today. Practice as though each time was your first time so that it doesn't become habitual. Keep yourself in the present moment by being fully aware of what is happening with the breath and the body in each moment.

By practicing the exercises with breath awareness, you may begin to wonder if your mind is telling you that this particular exercise is too difficult, or if you have actually reached your current physical limit. Whenever I teach a class, I see myself as the facilitator or guide. Each person in the class has to take responsibility for his or her self, and all have to ultimately find their own way. I will share many techniques and exercises with you, but ultimately you will need to take it upon yourself to put them into practice and discover what works best for you.

Sometimes, your mind will get in your way. For example, you may be able to do a certain exercise on one day, and on another day you may be feeling under the weather or physically unable to do what you did before. If you go with what you *think* you can do, you may get into trouble or get injured. Always stay in the present moment by allowing the breath to be your guide and move into and out of each movement and posture slowly. If your mind is stuck in the past or future, you are not in the present. By practicing meditation, you will develop a sense of what it is to be in the present moment.

Compassion is also a huge part of yoga practice. We tend to be our own worst enemies. Through practicing meditation, you will learn more about yourself and your own particular mind chatter. Many people have more compassion for others than for themselves. It is important to develop compassion for yourself. As you practice, be gentle with yourself. Just as you have compassion for others, you should have compassion for yourself. Just as you want to help other people, you should feel you want to help yourself.

There is no competition in yoga. It's all about discovering, observing, and having compassion for yourself. Go to the point where you feel the stretch and have self-acceptance that this is where you are. You will learn and discover so many things about yourself. Each person is unique, and each person's journey is different.

Here are a few key elements to always keep in mind as you move through the exercises:

- Listen to your breath.
- Listen to your body.
- Observe your mind with non-attachment.

In Kripalu yoga, we have a similar mantra, which is (BRFWA):

- Breathe
- Relax
- Feel
- Watch
- Allow

As we practice, it is important to come in and out of each posture with full awareness. Allow yourself to take several full, relaxing breaths into each one of your stretches and postures. Staying focused on your breath will allow you to stay connected with what is happening in your body.

Traditionally, one would practice yoga postures (*asanas*) to get the body ready for meditation. If the body has been stretched, strengthened, and moved, it is easier for the mind to be in meditation.

Through practicing these exercises based on yoga techniques, you can develop an awareness of breath and body that will help enrich your musical performance and overall well-being. For example, many musicians get very nervous before an audition or performance. I know of seasoned professionals who have resorted to taking beta-blockers or other drugs to reduce their anxiety before a performance. Practicing yoga prior to a performance can greatly reduce anxiety and enhance your performance.

Often, the exercises or postures we don't like end up being the ones we need the most. It is something to think about....

CHAPTER 1

Making Music with Yoga

As a performer, there are many expectations and pressures put upon you. You are expected to be at the top of your game all of the time. And who can always feel at their best? I think that is why so many artists crash. It is impossible to be at your best all of the time. We are only human. Knowing this and accepting this, we can lighten up on ourselves and bring the spontaneity and freedom back to our playing.

At one point in my life, I was feeling stuck and not very creative as a musician. I tried various ways to see if I could get that spark back, but nothing seemed to work. I decided to take a different approach and connect with another creative outlet that I used to enjoy doing: painting. I decided to take a couple of art courses to reconnect with my art. It was a wonderful experience, as I had no identity ties to this creativity. Since my identity and my need to make a living were not attached to the outcome, I was able to explore and be free in this creative expression.

Returning to art opened up my creative flow again, and I was able to take what I learned from this experience and connect with my musical creativity on another level. I realized that if I created and expressed myself with non-attachment, I could discover and do wonderful things. In art, I wasn't attached to the outcome. I was the observer and the explorer. I was then able to carry this into my music and have a similar sense of non-attachment and tap into that creative flow without worries or judgment about whether it was good or bad.

Non-attachment is being in the moment, doing what you have to do right now, without any expectations of how it should be. It is being in the present, not thinking about your past or your future. Be here right now. If you are attached to the outcome, it can hinder your objectivity and creativity immensely. If you are hoping for something, it takes you out of the present moment and puts you into the future. When you have a tough passage of music to play and you hope that it will come out, it brings up mind chatter and expectations.

What if you decided to be present in the music that is happening, and when it is your time to play, you are totally present in the moment, and play your heart out? This is non-attachment. You just do it.

This is where yoga blends with making music. Through practicing yoga, you actually practice non-attachment by becoming the observer of your thoughts. You detach yourself by stepping back and watching the thoughts. This thought watching is an important part of the practice. In meditation you learn to be the observer and watch your thoughts rather than allowing yourself to be carried away with the thoughts and getting wrapped up in all of the stories.

When we practice balancing exercises for focus and concentration, we immediately can see the flood of thoughts and judgments that try to take us away from our focus. When we perform, we have similar thoughts that will distract us. We will learn techniques to help us manage this mind chatter so that when we perform, we can stay fully present in the performance and play our best.

When you are the performer, your only task in that moment is to perform. You learn not to absorb all of the mind chatter and thoughts about the past or the future. You are set to a task in this moment. Focus on the now. "This is what I need to do." All you need to do is play; nothing else matters around you. That is your only task in this moment. Be fully present in this moment.

In yoga, we practice watching our thoughts and mind chatter, and we practice detachment from these thoughts, feelings, and emotions. We allow these things to come, but we watch them drift by us or let them pass through us. We begin to realize that we are not our thoughts, feelings, or emotions. We learn to have patience with ourselves and to be kind to ourselves. We discover that we are usually our own worst enemies. By practicing yoga, we can learn to develop patience and be kind to ourselves. This compassion towards ourselves is really important to develop throughout all of these exercises.

I enjoy performing in different ensembles. The whole notion of an ensemble is to play together. Let's face it, it is always more enjoyable to play with people who are supportive of each other and to go on stage as a team. When it is anything less than this, playing in ensembles can become a negative experience. If there is a sense of competition or rivalry, it tends to be less fun for you and the audience, whereas if all of the performers are on the same team, it is much more enjoyable for everyone.

In yoga, we greet each other and end our classes by saying "*Namaste*," which means, "I see the light within you." It is a lovely expression where we honor the good in each other. Having this positive outlook when you see others is a wonderful way to address each other and our audiences. Even if you don't actually say it out loud, you can think it.

Playing music should be a positive experience rather than a negative, competitive experience. We should learn to support ourselves and each other. Imagine if we greeted our fellow musicians with this "*Namaste*." How would that change the way we work and play with other people? What if you would greet your audience with this? If we honor the goodness in all, we can bring that forth in all that we do.

As musicians, we can find ourselves in various performing situations. We may be sitting in with a band for one function, or we may have a regular group of musicians we play with most of the time. Whatever the situation is, it is always nice if you can feel like you are all going on stage and are making music together. It should feel like it is a group effort. We are all in this together. I have found that different groups of musicians do different things before they go on stage. Some bands pray together before they play, some drink, and some do yoga. It is such a wonderful experience to play with other musicians when you have group effort and you all support each other.

It is an amazing experience to play with people you can really connect with. I had a particularly exceptional performance experience when I was invited to teach a *Musician's Yoga* seminar at an international music festival and was also invited to be a featured flute soloist for the final performance. The students had full days of rehearsals and classes, so I was not sure how many people would actually participate in the yoga seminar. To my surprise and delight, all of the students and faculty at this festival showed up and were eager to learn and to participate. We had an enjoyable afternoon together breathing, stretching, and learning yoga techniques to help for performance and daily life. When it came time for the performance, I felt that I had really connected with these people, and it made the performance so much richer. I was calm, centered, and happy to share my music with everybody. It is truly an extraordinary opportunity to be able to practice yoga with people that you perform with. There is a shared sense of openness and trust.

Several of my students have introduced these yoga techniques to their fellow band members, and now they all practice yoga together in their rehearsals and before they go on stage. Yoga means union. It can bring people together as well as bring the mind and body together.

VISUALIZING PERFORMANCE SUCCESS

🧘 Here's a scenario in which practicing yoga could help your music performance. Imagine that you have to go on stage to play one piece for an international festival, and the concert is filled with high profile musicians. What would you do if you start to get nervous? What if you visualized yourself backstage, listening to the others before you, and started feeling insecure? It could be for a number of reasons, but somehow, you are having doubts about performing.

What if someone sensed your insecurity and said that you don't really have to perform, if you really don't want to? What would you do? Would you say to yourself, "Whew, I am glad someone noticed," and not perform? Or would you say to yourself, "I can't miss this opportunity. I really need to play, no matter how I feel."

How would you have felt after the experience? Would you have regretted missing this opportunity if you didn't do it?

What if you decided to go for it, and put your heart into the music and into the present moment and played like you never played before? What if you decided to play but stayed focused on your feelings and let your nerves get the best of you? How much energy would have been wasted in engaging all of the mind chatter? And, how much energy would have been left for the music? 🧘

There is this "what if" factor that we have when we come to a performance. We all know the mind chatter that creates anxiety. Inner voices tell you that you are inadequate in some way. What if I go on stage and mess it up? What if some famous musician is in the audience listening to me? What if I forget my music? What if I start shaking? What if there are a lot of people in the audience? What if there are very few people? The list can go on and on.

These "what ifs" are the mind chatter that can create a whole chain of anxiety. If you allow the mind to focus on the mind chatter, you can become so distracted that you will be unable to perform at your best. By practicing yoga and meditation, you will be able to clear the mind chatter so that you will be able to focus on your performance.

What if you took all of those "what ifs" and turned them into something positive? Like, "I am so happy that this famous musician came to see me perform. I am so happy to have this experience to play for so many people." If we turn the negative mind chatter into a positive, our performances will become much more enjoyable to us and to our audiences. What we feel gets projected into our music.

What if you were able to be so in the moment that you were not able to focus on the "what ifs" and were able to stay fully present in your performance? What if you went on stage and it was a great experience?

Yoga and meditation can help you clear the mind chatter. That is how you can blend yoga techniques with performance techniques. These are the things we will focus on in this book.

What if you did stop yourself and never gave yourself a chance? Just because you are nervous is no reason to stop yourself. You grow when you step out and rise to the occasion. You get better with practice and experience. Yoga is a tool to help you develop a one-pointed focus and concentration. It teaches you to stay in the present moment. Through practicing yoga and meditation, you will begin to realize that you are not your feelings. Through visualization, you can imagine yourself in various performance experiences and practice trying to have positive outcomes in different scenarios.

If you always go by what you are feeling, you may end up not doing very much. Practicing meditation will teach you to separate yourself from your thoughts. When you practice meditation, you begin to watch your thoughts and realize that you are not your thoughts or feelings. You learn to find your center, and realize that no one else can touch this center. And, no matter where you go, this center is always with you, and it is you. It is separate from your thoughts and feelings. You learn that no matter what situation you find yourself in, that this center *is* you.

When you are in a situation such as a competition or where you know you are being judged, you may feel anxious about your performance. If you visualize, in your practice time, that the adjudicators want the best for you and that you are going to give your best and share your talents, you can come into the performance with a positive attitude and perform your best. Before you arrived, you would have already imagined what it would be like and feel like to be in this situation. So, you are preparing yourself and your mind—actually practicing for the event, rather than "hoping" it will go well.

Get in touch with why you like to play. Making music is a gift, and it should be enjoyable for both you and your audience, no matter who that audience is.

Do you find yourself in different types of performing experiences? I have found myself in so many various experiences that sometimes I love to play and other times I wonder why I am playing. Playing should be enjoyable. After all, isn't that why you wanted to make music in the first place?

If you are not having fun or are really nervous, chances are that your audience will pick up on this negative energy, and your performance will not be its best. On the other hand, if you are enjoying yourself, chances are that your audience will be able to enjoy themselves more and be able to pick up on your positive energy.

Yoga can help with nervous energy. By practicing breathing and meditation techniques, you will be able to calm and center yourself and learn how to separate yourself from the negative thoughts and mind chatter. Through meditating, you figure out what you need to work on and what your problems are. You become more aware of how your mind works and how you can watch your thoughts. Through practicing meditation with your music, you can see how your mind works when you get in different performance situations, and you can be able to control your mind chatter, calm your nerves, and enjoy performing.

I had the experience of being the observer of all of the back stage chaos at an international conference. Instead of being in the performer's seat, I was asked to be the photographer for a group of very high-profile musicians who were performing.

It was an interesting experience to be on the other side, being the observer of all of the different personalities backstage, rather than being in the performer's seat. This whole experience was like thought watching. I wasn't wrapped up in the outcome of any of the performances. Even though this backstage scene has always been around me, I was able to see the situation with different eyes. As the photographer, I was able to step back and take it all in. It was interesting to observe how all of the musicians reacted to this chaos before they went on stage.

Some of the musicians were by themselves, warming up on their instrument, focusing on what they had to do before they went on stage. Some were focusing and meditating in their own way, looking distant from all of the activity around them. Others were anxiously talking and trying to make conversation. From the observer's point of view, I saw how each of these musicians dealt with the anticipation of preparing to go on stage. I was actually able to really feel distant and just observe in this situation. I was also able to be more aware and observe how others handled the stress and what they did just minutes before going on stage. This kind of detached analysis should be one of the goals of practice. The difference is that you look at yourself, rather than at others.

In my yoga classes, I always tell my students that we are here to connect with ourselves and not to worry about what anybody else is doing or what they can do or what we cannot do. I always tell them that there is no room for judges in the room when we practice yoga. It is important not to let the mind get in the way, where we push ourselves past our limits. When you practice, it is time to notice what is happening in your body and mind, and not judge it. You become the observer. Practicing yoga is practicing awareness and mindfulness. We learn to develop the mind-body connection and watch our thoughts.

By practicing meditation, we learn to observe the mind chatter. We learn to observe it and embrace it. You will probably find a lot of mind chatter when you are preparing for a performance or are playing a concert. All of the "what if?" scenarios start to flood the mind. Visualization is a big part of meditation. Visualize different performance spaces, different audiences, different situations, and put a positive spin on what you practice.

VISUALIZATION EXERCISES

🧘 Visualize yourself going on stage, and imagine filling the room with your presence. Have the feeling that the audience has come because they want to hear you play. Think positive thoughts. Visualize yourself being relaxed and calm, as in meditation. Imagine you are in an audition and the jury is vigorously writing or even whispering to each other. Visualize this happening, because very often, it does. How would you feel? What would the mind chatter be? Can you still stay present and play your best without getting upset or letting it distract you? Can you visualize yourself playing your best and imagine they were writing and whispering wonderful things about your performance?

Try to see the positive rather than the negative. How would your world change if you saw things from the positive side? One little shift in perception can change your world. Thinking a different way can open you up to new possibilities and new opportunities. Visualize yourself playing for an audience of 3,000 people. Can you imagine feeling excited that all of these people came to hear you play? Can you visualize being happy, and see and feel yourself enjoying this experience? ♟

One of my students would get so nervous that she would talk to everyone around her before going on stage. She was uncomfortable with the silence. Can you practice being with this silence and learn to enjoy it? Visualize yourself going on stage and listening to the silence. Listen for the silence and the power of the silence. When musicians get energized, they tend to overplay or rush through their performance. Imagine listening to the silence on stage so that you won't overplay when you improvise or rush through your music. Imagine that you had all of the time in the world to play your piece. Enjoy each moment. This can be a wonderful meditation to practice. Practice listening to the silence and the space in the music. Mozart and Miles both share this kind of artistry in their music.

PUT IT INTO PRACTICE

♟ A good meditation is to imagine getting in touch with your emotions before a performance. If you feel excited about performing, then it's important to review the following affirmation.

Do you feel doubtful or anxious, and if so, can you imagine feeling the stage lights and being positive and enjoying it? If you can get the feeling of being positive, then bask in the stage lights and enjoy yourself. If you are uncomfortable, let's see if you can change your outlook and feelings to let those nerves subside. Take a few moments to think about the following points, and feel it in your body and mind.

This is your time to enjoy your performance and express yourself. Say, "I am here to share my music with you."

We are all here to make music, and feelings and emotions will come and go. Enjoy the waves of emotions, and realize that your center is not affected.

Imagine being on stage. If you feel any nervousness, allow it to wash over you or pass through you. Do not let it absorb you, but see it as an emotion. It is a feeling. Enjoy the waves of emotions as they pass through you.

Think about how you will feel before the concert. Then, imagine how you will feel after the concert. You will probably feel differently. You are the same person, but your feelings have changed. You are not your feelings. ♟

CHAPTER 2

Breathing Techniques (*Pranayama*)

"One thing I noticed is that when I was playing, especially the more high-energy music, I held my breath. Meditating and yoga have allowed me to recognize this and to remedy it. By being able to control the breath, I've increased my stamina, and also, my arms aren't cramping up as they used to. I recently had an experience where I used the breath not only to calm my nerves, but to focus and perform my best."

The breath is the key to practicing yoga. Without focusing on the breath, you are just stretching and not doing yoga. Why is the breath so important? Without breath, you do not have life! When we become anxious or nervous, our breath is the first to go. It becomes shallow, short, and fast.

To immediately center yourself and be in the present moment, simply bring awareness to your breath, and begin to deepen it. If you take in a deep breath and exhale it away with an audible sigh, you can immediately bring yourself to the present moment. The sound of the sigh will help relieve stress, and focusing on the exhale can release tension. Simply doing a few sighs can help ground you and bring you back to your center.

We will learn how to do the **full yogic breath**, which is the foundation of our breathing techniques. But first, it is important to know that there are many forms of breaths that we practice in the yoga tradition to get different results. Some breaths will calm us and others will energize us. Some will do both.

Learning these different breathing techniques will help you in different situations. These techniques help you regulate and change your energy, outlook, mood, and spirit. By concentrating on the breath, we connect the body with the mind. By connecting breathing techniques with meditation and visualization, we can create many various ways to help us enhance our performance and make it enjoyable for ourselves and for our audience. Learning these techniques will help with your breath support, musical phrasing, concentration, focus, and relaxation. It will help calm those nerves. Connecting with the breath also connects the body and the mind. It is a key element to practicing yoga and to practicing your instrument.

CALMING BREATHS BACKSTAGE

I was once working with some students backstage before they went on for a big performance that was being recorded for national television. Some of them were very nervous about this experience. I gave them various calming breaths and exercises that they could do before and during their performance so they could center themselves. We worked with breathing techniques such as sighing, taking a long, slow breath, making the exhales longer than the inhales, and visualizing. They were able to stay focused and played beautifully.

Even if you only have two seconds, you can use yoga to release tension: Take in a big breath, and then exhale it with an audible sigh.

BREATH RECOGNITION EXERCISE

🧘 To get in touch with how you breathe, try this simple exercise. Start by lying on your back. Rest your hands on your belly with fingertips slightly touching and loosely interlaced. Notice what happens to your hands as you gently breathe in and out. Don't try to change your breath, just notice. You should notice that your hands will move slightly towards each other as you exhale and your hands will slightly separate as you inhale, allowing more room for breath to expand the rib cage. This expansion of the breath in the rib cage happens as you press the diaphragm downward, so that the belly expands slightly. This is our natural breath. 🧘

A wonderful image to have in mind while you are working with breath is to think of the whole rib cage area as a balloon. When you blow up a balloon, you are expanding it—just as when you inhale deeply, you are expanding your rib cage. Some musicians have what is called "reversed breathing." In reversed breathing, you are not actually able to get a deep, full breath because of a mistaken belief that to get a deep breath, you have to draw the muscles of the abdomen in and tense up the shoulders when you inhale and relax these muscles on the exhale. The truth is exactly the opposite.

Lying on your back is the most natural position to feel your breath. Once you feel comfortable with this natural breath, you can start to practice the **full yogic breath**—which is just an expansion of our natural breath—in a seated and a standing position. This breath will be the basis for all of the breath work and exercises that you will be learning.

BREATHE THROUGH THE NOSE

In practicing breathing techniques, always inhale and exhale through the nose, unless otherwise specified. Your mouth should be closed. Whether you are practicing yoga or not, it is much healthier to breathe through the nose, as it functions as a filter system for your lungs.

FULL YOGIC BREATH (THREE-PART *DIRGHA* BREATH)

The most important breath to get familiar with is the **full yogic breath**. It is our foundational breath, just as the **mountain pose** (see p. 45) is our foundational posture. Practice the **full yogic breath** until it becomes natural.

The **full yogic breath**, or three-part *dirgha* breath, is a willful breath. To practice this breath, we will take our normal breath as explained above and expand and deepen it, filling up the belly, rib cage, and all the way up to the collarbone.

It is traditionally described in these three parts, but ultimately, it should feel like a long, slow, deep breath in, and a long, slow exhale out.

We will practice this breath in three positions. First of all, we will practice on our backs, as that is the easiest way to get in touch with our natural breath. It is also safer to start here. If you are not used to taking long, slow, deep breaths, you may get dizzy in the beginning. If you ever feel dizzy in any of the exercises, you can always regulate your system by lying on the ground. Once you have learned the breaths on your back, explore the breath in a seated position and also in a standing position. Since the **full yogic breath** is the most important breath, take the time to really work with it and really feel it.

Full Yogic Breath: Lying on Your Back

🧘 Start this exercise as above, lying on your back with your hands resting on your belly, fingertips slightly touching and loosely interlaced. Get in touch with your natural breath by noticing the breath just as it is, moving in and out of the body. Notice where the breath goes when you breathe in, and notice how it is released from the body as you breathe out. Once you get a sense of this, start to deepen the breath gradually.

1. **Belly.** The first part of the breath is the belly. To come into the first part of the breath, start with the exhale. The next time you exhale, start to actively draw the muscles of the abdomen in and up towards the spine, squeezing out the air with these muscles. The hands come together slightly. Once the air is squeezed out, relax the muscles of the abdomen to allow the breath to fill up the lower rib cage, which pushes on the abdomen to expand the belly. You will notice that your hands will separate slightly as in the first exercise. Try this for a few rounds of breath, repeating this process until it becomes comfortable.

2. **Rib Cage.** The second part of the breath is the rib cage. Inhale and expand the breath again, but beyond allowing the breath to fill the belly, draw in more breath so that you feel the rib cage expand in the front, back, and sides of your body. Try placing your hands on the sides of the rib cage to feel the expansion on the sides of the body. Also try keeping one hand on the belly and sliding the other hand under the back, so you can feel the front and back of the body expanding as well. Continue to actively use your abdominal muscles to expel the breath on an exhale. Relax these muscles to allow the breath to come in, filling up the belly and the rib cage. Practice breathing into these two parts (belly and rib cage) until you can really feel it.

3. **Collarbone.** The third part of the breath is to breathe up to the collarbone. When you are ready to inhale, relax the abdominal muscles to expand the belly and the rib cage, but this time, sip in even more air to fill up to the top of the lungs. Place one hand just under the collarbone to feel a slight lift in this area. This is the subtlest of the three parts, as you will only be able to feel a slight movement here.

Continue to breathe into all three parts, coming into one long, slow, deep, full breath. Exhale fully as you squeeze the abdominal muscles in and up towards the spine. Then inhale fully as you relax the abdominal muscles, filling up the entire rib cage. Think about smoothing these three parts into one breath.

Though the **full yogic breath** is a willful breath, see if you can bring some softness to your effort. You should be feeling quite relaxed, at this point.

Full Yogic Breath in a Seated Position

Once you feel comfortable doing the **full yogic breath** while lying on your back, you can try it in a seated position. It is important to come into this breath gradually. Find a comfortable seated position either in a chair with your feet flat on the ground and hip-width apart, or in a cross-legged position sitting on the floor. Keep your spine elongated, your shoulders relaxed down and back, and your shoulder blades drawing slightly towards each other as the chest lifts slightly. Lift slightly from the crown of the head, visualizing a string attached to it, elongating the spine, creating space between each of the vertebrae.

Start the same sequence that you did lying on your back. Starting with an exhale, squeeze the air out, then relax the muscles of the abdomen, allowing the air to fill up the belly, the rib cage, and all the way up to the collarbone.

If you feel dizzy, back away, and come back to a soft, normal breath. You can also lie back on the floor and come back to a normal breath to regain your equilibrium.

Full Yogic Breath in a Standing Position

Once you feel comfortable doing a **full yogic breath** in a seated position, you are ready to try it in a standing position.

Come into a standing position with your feet hip-width apart and parallel. Keep a slight bend in the knees. Tuck the tailbone under slightly. Relax the shoulders back and down. Elongate from the crown of the head (this is **mountain pose**). I like to imagine a helium balloon attached to the top of my head. Another image is to imagine a string attached to the top of your head with all of the bones dangling on this string, stacking up beautifully, with no effort. Connect with your natural breath, then start to deepen it, as you did in the lying down and seated positions, by drawing your abdominal muscles in and up towards your spine, squeezing all of the air out of the rib cage. Then, relax the abdominal muscles, allowing the breath to fill up the belly and rib cage, and sip in a little more air to fill all the way up to the collarbone while maintaining relaxation in the shoulders. Continue with this breath until it becomes fluid and natural. 🧘

It is important to use this full breath with all the warm-up exercises and postures. This is our main source of connection with the body and mind. It is our guide to indicate whether we are forcing too much in our stretches and postures. If you cannot keep a full breath flowing at all times, you have either lost your focus on the breath, or you have come too deep into a stretch and need to back away to be able to keep a deep-flowing breath.

When you learn to consciously deepen your breath with the **full yogic breath**, you will immediately be able to bring your attention to the present moment and relax your mind and body.

OCEAN BREATH (*UJJAYI*)

The ocean-sounding breath is added to the **full yogic breath**. It helps the mind focus on the sound of the breath. This sound gives the mind another concrete point to focus on during meditation and while you are in the postures, and therefore increases concentration. The ocean sound is produced by *lightly* constricting the muscles of the back of the throat. It is a very calming, relaxing, and centering breath.

🧘 To practice the **ocean breath**, pretend that you are fogging a mirror, creating a warm sound. Produce this same sound, but close the lips. You will feel that the muscles in the back of the throat are lightly constricted. Keep this light constriction both on the exhalation and the inhalation. Once you get the sound, begin to relax the area of the throat more so that you are not creating tension. It should be a very subtle, relaxing sound.

When you get the feel for this sound, start to practice it with the **full yogic breath**. Begin by coming into the **full yogic breath**, then add the ocean-sounding breath as you are ready. Breathe long, slow, deep breaths. Allow your mind to stay focused on the sound of the ocean, allowing the waves of sound to wash over you, back and forth. ♣

ALTERNATE NOSTRIL BREATHING (*NADI SHODHANA*)

Alternate nostril breathing is one of the most relaxing and calming breaths there is. It helps to balance the right and left hemispheres of the brain, creating a sense of peace and centeredness. It is helpful to practice this breath right before you go on stage or into an audition. It is also helpful to practice this to fully relax the mind and body before going to bed.

♣ Start this breath in a comfortable seated position with your spine tall and shoulders relaxed. Connect with your breath, then come into the **full yogic breath** gradually. When you are fully connected with the **full yogic breath**, you can begin **alternate nostril breathing**. You can either use your right or left hand, but I will describe it using the right hand, as this is the traditional way it is taught.

With your right hand, gently place your first (pointer) and second (middle) fingers between your eyebrows, and slightly higher. This is the third eye point. Just pressing on this third eye point gently can stimulate calmness.

Start the breath by exhaling all of your air. Close the right nostril with your thumb and inhale through your left nostril. Close your left nostril with your ring finger, then release your thumb and exhale through your right nostril. Inhale through the right nostril, closing this nostril, then exhale through the left side. Inhale through the left nostril, close, and exhale through the right nostril.

Continue with this breath from side to side in the same manner for at least two to five minutes. Keep the breath long and slow as you inhale one side, close, exhale to the other side, inhale this same side, close, and exhale to the other side. When you are ready to release the alternate nostril breath, the next time you exhale through the left nostril, allow the hand to come back to your lap and rest it there. Come back to a normal, soft breath. Pause for a moment, and notice how you feel. ♟

CONDUCTOR BREATH

Conductor breath is a very energizing, uplifting breath. It is a great breath to use if you are feeling a little sluggish and need some extra energy. Practice it during a break at your rehearsals, or practice sessions to revive yourself. It is also a great breath to use to release tension in the upper body. I tell my students to try a few rounds of this breath to get the body going in the morning or to get you energized in the afternoon instead of running for the caffeine. Anytime you feel the need for a little energy, give this one a try.

♟ Start this breath in a standing position. Make sure that your legs are a little wider than hip-width apart, and keep your knees slightly bent. This breath is done with three inhales through the nose and one exhale through the mouth with a "HAA" sound from deep within the belly.

With the first breath, inhale as you move the arms straight up overhead in front of the body; release the arms down by your sides. Then inhale as you move the arms straight out to the side. Release the arms down by your sides, then inhale the arms straight up in front of the body again. Exhale with a "HAA" breath, bending forward halfway towards the ground, or as far as it feels comfortable, allowing the knees to bend a little deeper as the arms swing down beside your legs. Let the knees act as a spring to bring you back up into standing and right into the next round, swinging the arms overhead with an inhale, arms out to the side with an inhale, arms overhead with an inhale, and bending forward with a "HAA" exhale.

Swing back up, and continue with this sequence, drawing in energy on the inhalations and letting go of anything you no longer need—whether it be a thought, emotion, feeling, or tension—on the "HAA" exhale. Use the inhale to energize, and use the exhale to let go. You can also turn the corners of your mouth up just slightly, and notice how that can change your energy as well.

Repeat this sequence in a fluid, steady motion 3 to 10 times. When you finish, come back to standing, and exhale it away with a sigh. Pause here for a few relaxing breaths to connect back with your center, and notice how you feel in this moment.

If you have any lower back sensitivity, or if it does not feel good for your head to come down so low, you can regulate the depth of this breath by not bending forward so much. You can come down halfway or even part of the way. ♟

HELICOPTER BREATH

Helicopter breath is a combination of helicopter (see p. 63) with an energizing breath. It loosens up the arms, shoulders, and spine. It uplifts your mood and spirit, and it balances the entire body. **Helicopter breath** is one of the best breaths to practice daily, as it keeps the upper body loose and relaxed. As you practice this breath, visualize that you are allowing all of the tension in your upper back, shoulders, arms, wrists, hands, and fingers to flow out the arms and release through the fingertips.

♟ Begin with the **helicopter** movement. Stand with your feet a little wider than hip-width apart. Keep the knees slightly bent to protect the knees and lower back. Allow the arms to relax down by your side. Then, start turning your torso from side to side. As you turn from side to side, look over each shoulder, bringing the twist from the base of the spine all the way to the crown of the head. Allow the arms to relax fully as they flop back and forth.

Start to increase the tempo as you twist the spine from side to side. The arms should be so relaxed that they simply flop from side to side, hitting whatever part of the body they may, as the torso turns from side to side. Find a speed that works well for you. Some days, you may want to do the motion faster; other days, you may want to slow it down. This movement really loosens up the upper body and gets the blood flowing.

The next step is to add the breath to this movement to create more energy and release tension. Every time you pass through the center of your body, inhale through the nose. Every time you come to each side, exhale through the mouth with a "HAA" breath, from deep within the belly. To create more energy, really drink in the breath through the nose. To release tension, concentrate on the deep belly "HAA" sound on each side. Bring the corners of the mouth up just slightly, and notice how that can also change your mood and energy level.

Practice this about 30 seconds to a minute, then start to release the breath, coming back to a normal breath, and slow down the movement gradually, finding your way back to stillness at center. Pause at center when you have come to a complete stop, and notice how you feel.

You may feel a little dizzy; that is normal. If you keep your eyes focused straight ahead on a single point (a *drishdi*), the dizziness should subside more quickly. You will probably feel a natural "high." Just notice. If at any point you feel very dizzy, come to the floor and relax. You may be pushing yourself too much. You can also practice this exercise without the "HAA" breath, or simply do a less vigorous breath if that feels more appropriate for you. ♣

PUT IT INTO PRACTICE

No matter what results you are trying to achieve, practicing different breathing techniques will help you connect with your breath more. Connecting to your breath can help many aspects of musicianship, including better tone production for your instrument, allowing your music and phrases to breathe, reducing tension and stress, and calming your nerves.

Once you have learned these breathing exercises, you will find various situations where they are especially useful. As you may have already discovered, each breath yields different results. Depending upon how much time you have and what results you want to achieve, there are various breaths that you can practice. I have listed various situations for using these breathing exercises.

♣ Have a few seconds and need a quick fix to calm you down? A simple inhale and exhale with a sigh can immediately calm, center, and ground you.

♣ Need to relax and center yourself for a performance or an audition?
Come into the **full yogic breath** to center yourself. Once this is established, come into the **alternate nostril breathing**.

🧘 Need more energy?
   Try 5 to 10 **conductor breaths**.

🧘 Need to relax the upper body, neck, and shoulders and feel energized? Try a few minutes of the **helicopter** movement with the **helicopter breath**.

🧘 Practice awareness of your breath throughout the day and throughout the week. What are some of your observations? 🧘

Breathing Techniques

Breath	Benefits	Page
Full Yogic Breath (Three Part *Dirgha* Breath)	basic breath for developing awareness	12
Ocean Breath (*Ujjayi*)	brings focus and concentration on the breath, calms, relaxes and centers us	15
Alternate Nostril Breathing (*Nadi Shodhana*)	very calming and relaxing	16
Conductor Breath	very energizing and uplifting	17
Helicopter Breath	very energizing and balancing	18

CHAPTER 3

Meditation
Techniques

"In the beginning of the semester, taking ten minutes out of each day to meditate didn't seem like a good use of the limited time available. However, after consistently forcing myself to take a step back and detach, I've found increased mental strength and stability."

THOUGHT WATCHING

🧘 Before reading this chapter, pause for one minute, close your eyes, and just notice all of the thoughts that come and go in a matter of one minute. Set a timer so that you know how long one minute is. Just give it a try. It's only one minute!

So, how many thoughts did you have? What were your thoughts about? Were you surprised at how long one minute actually was? Were you surprised at how many thoughts you had in one minute? Was there one particular thought that kept coming back? ♟

Meditation is one of the harder practices to do because the mind's nature is to be active at all times. When I first started to meditate, I would wonder if I was doing it "right," because my mind would never stop. I kept getting frustrated, wondering how I was ever going to stop my thoughts so that I could get down to business and meditate. Thinking I was missing something, I would try various practices, still with no luck. After some time and more training, I began to realize that the mind is always in this state of activity. In meditation, we are not trying to stop or push our thoughts away. We are trying to become the witness or observer of our thoughts. The more we try to stop our thoughts or push our thoughts away, the more frequent and intense they become.

By practicing meditation, we learn to focus the mind for increased concentration and relaxation. In meditation, we use a particular focus for the mind so that when a thought comes, it can pass through us, move over us, or go around us. Our job is to keep our focus in the forefront at all times. If a thought tries to grab our attention and carry us away into a particular story, we simply notice whenever this happens and then bring our attention back to our focus.

I enjoy sailing, so I like to imagine that every thought that comes to me is on a sailboat. I watch that sailboat float right on by, rather than jumping into it and being carried away with that particular thought. Some days there are many sailboats and the wind is fast and furious. Other days, there are fewer boats and gentler breezes. Many times, I find myself on a sailboat, being carried away with a particular thought. When I realize that it's happening, I acknowledge without judgment that I got on the boat, and was carried away with that thought. I then get off that boat, letting the thought go with the boat. I let it drift on by without getting upset that I "failed" again.

Try listening to music this way, with this feeling of non-attachment. Does it sound different to you?

Meditation is the process of letting go time after time, becoming the observer of our thoughts—realizing that we are not our thoughts. This practice of non-attachment is what we do in meditation. The more we practice, the more we will find those brief times of silence as the mind becomes quieter. We begin to connect with our center.

I can't emphasize enough that you should not push those thoughts away. If you try, they will become more intense and you will become more frustrated. Let them come, let them all come, then simply let them go. Let them float right on by.... I have a friend who visualizes thoughts as waves passing through his body. Whatever way you want to think of it is fine.

Witness your thoughts rather than become your thoughts or feelings. Do not become your thoughts. The more you detach yourself from your thoughts, the more you will realize that you are not your thoughts. Be the observer of the thought, do not become the thought or attach yourself to the thought. This is an excellent practice of trying to become compassionate with yourself rather than being self-judgmental. Become the witness, not the judge. There are many, many ways to say the same thing.

Meditation may be practiced in many different ways and for different lengths of time, sitting still or moving. Different meditations produce different results, especially if we combine them with visualization. I will share with you some traditional meditation techniques and show you how to apply these techniques to your music. You can do a brief meditation, less than one minute long, before you go on stage. Or, you can practice longer meditations over time, such as when you are preparing for a concert.

The whole idea is to use the meditation and visualization principles to achieve more accurate performance results. It is important to meditate on what you set out to do in a performance so that you actually accomplish your goals.

When we practice meditation, we have a particular focus in mind. The focus may be on the breath, a word, or a mantra. It can be a visual focus such as a candle flame, a tactile focus like counting the beads of a mala or rosary, a focus on the sound of our instrument, or a focus on the steady rhythm of our scales. We can become so focused that we lose track of time and get lost in the experience.

We will be focusing on different types of traditional yoga meditations in this chapter: breath meditation, mantra meditation, counting meditation, and meditation in motion. With each traditional form of meditation, we will explore ways to incorporate your instrumental and musical practice with these traditional meditation practices. We will also explore how to use visualization with meditation to create specific results.

By practicing meditation, we learn how to focus our attention and our mind so that we will be able to concentrate and bring our attention to the present moment and give our best as we play our instrument and live our daily lives.

Through practicing meditation and visualization, you can pave your way to a positive experience. Your outlook will change dramatically. Practicing meditation helps to develop your focus and center. Practicing visualization will help bring you closer to your goals.

SET A TIMER

It is helpful to set a timer, alarm clock, or the alarm on your computer or phone with a pleasant sound to take you out of meditation. That way, you can totally relax and be in meditation without worrying that you will lose track of time. The idea is that you don't have to think or worry about anything. It is pretty hard to be in the present moment if you keep looking at the clock, wondering when your 10-minute meditation is going to be over.

BREATH MEDITATION

We start our meditation practice with basic breath awareness, since this is the key element to focusing the mind and bringing our attention to the present moment.

The breath meditation is our foundation for all of the other meditations. Bringing your attention to the breath is the quickest way to bring your attention to the present moment. For example, take in a deep breath, and exhale with a long audible sigh. This will help immediately ground you in the present moment and also release stress and tension. If you only have a moment before you go on stage, just try this simple sigh. It can help ground and center you immediately and also release any unwanted tension.

🧘 To start a basic breath meditation, find a *comfortable* seated position with your spine tall, shoulders relaxed, face and jaw soft. I cannot emphasize the word "comfortable" enough. If sitting on the floor in a cross-legged position is comfortable for you, then do it. If it is not, then find another position, such as sitting at the edge of a chair with your feet flat on the floor and hip-width apart. The most important thing is that you can sit in this position for at least 5 to 10 minutes without getting distracted that your back or legs are hurting. If sitting nice and tall is difficult for you, that just means that you need to practice in shorter segments, to begin to strengthen those muscles that are used to keep you in this upright position. You may also want to try sitting up against the wall so that the back has more support, in the beginning. Make sure that the buttocks are up against the wall and that the shoulder blades and back of the head are touching the wall, with the chin parallel to the floor.

With the spine tall and shoulders relaxed, lengthen a bit more from the crown of your head. Imagine a helium balloon attached to the crown of the head, bringing more space between the vertebrae. Allow your hands to rest on your lap. If you would like to feel more grounded, place the palms facing down. If you would like more energy, face the palms up. Close your eyes or have a soft gaze in front of you. Bring your attention to the present moment by noticing all of the sounds around you. Allow your ear to jump from sound to sound. Notice the sounds in the room at first, then expand your awareness to include the sounds outside of the room. Resist the urge to identify the source of the sounds. Also resist the urge to label a particular sound as good or bad. Just notice without judgment.

Now, release the sounds, and bring your attention to the body sitting on the chair or floor. Notice the point of contact beneath you. What is actually touching? Notice the length in the spine and feel the crown of the head lifting slightly as you root through the sitting bones. Begin to scan your body, and notice any areas of tightness or holding. Bring your attention to these areas, and see if you can release, relax, and let go, softening the muscles of these areas.

Release the sensations in your body, and bring your attention to the breath. Without changing the breath, notice the quality of the breath. Is it long or short, deep or shallow? Then start to lengthen the breath. You don't have to come into the full three-part yogic breath, but you can at first, if that helps you to connect with the breath more. Continue focusing your attention on the breath. Whenever you notice that the mind is wandering or you lose track of the breath, just notice that it happened, and bring your attention back to the breath. Keep the breath in the forefront of your focus and awareness, no matter what thoughts may arise. 🧘

At times, you may feel that the mind has become calmer and you can feel that centeredness—that grounding feeling, the feeling of calmness and peacefulness. Rather than reaching for this goal and trying to attain this feeling, simply watch it and notice it, just as with any other thought or feeling that may come. Practicing meditation will help you bring full attention to whatever task is at hand, which is, of course, very helpful when you are performing. You want to be fully present and give your best.

BREATH MEDITATION WITH YOUR INSTRUMENT

Many musicians hold their breath or otherwise do not breathe with musical phrases. This is especially true of musicians who play instruments that don't require breath to produce the sound, such as pianists, guitarists, string players, and percussionists.

Whether you play one of these instruments or you are a singer or a wind player, it is of the utmost importance for you as a musician to know how to breathe properly and be able to produce musical phrases by using the breath.

♟ Once you have the feeling of the basic breath meditation, you can pick up your instrument and apply the same principles. Practice scales, long tones, rudiments, or any other instrumental technique as you concentrate on the breath and allow your instrumental practice to become a meditation. Focus on a steady, even breath.

Also, many musicians tend to hold their breath and tense up the body when they try to play fast or try to play a difficult passage. Concentrate on deepening the breath and relaxing as you play.

Try these techniques with music or scales that you feel comfortable with, so that you can be on automatic pilot while you concentrate on breathing. Start practicing with a piece or a scale that you already know, and play with a steady, even breath. Visualize that you are riding the breath. ♟

Experiment with this aspect for your individual instrument. Notice how you breathe when you play. Are you taking a full, deep breath, or are you tightening the muscles of the belly and shrugging your shoulders? Notice, and try to play with a full, relaxed breath.

MANTRA MEDITATION

Adding a mantra—a word, short phrase, or sound—to this basic breath meditation can also help focus your attention. It gives the mind another anchor. A mantra could be something as simple as saying to yourself "breath in" as you breathe in and "breath out" as you breathe out. It could also be a word or phrase of something that you wish to manifest, such as saying "peace" or "calm."

Traditionally, mantras came from Sanskrit, the ancient language of India. An ancient mantra you can try is "Ham Sa" (pronounced H-ah-m S-ah), which translates into "I am that I am." Say to yourself "Ham" on the in breath and "Sa" on the out breath. Or, you may say "I am" on the in breath and "that I am" on the out breath, if that feels more comfortable. You can also use any word or phrase that you like. The point is to have another word or sound that the mind can focus on in coordination with the breath.

When we practice mantra meditation with our instruments, we focus on the sound that we are producing as we play our instruments.

MANTRA MEDITATION WITH YOUR INSTRUMENT

We can focus our practice on listening to the sound of our instrument as we play our technical exercises and pieces. Be fully present and absorb yourself in the sound that you are creating with your instrument. Make the most beautiful sounds possible. Let them come out with ease. If you are looking for a particular type of sound as you play, focus on it. For instance, sometimes the sound needs to be full and rich, and sometimes you need to play with more openness. Whatever type of sound you are trying to produce, bring your full attention and focus on the sound as you play.

🧘 When there are too many things that you are trying to focus on at one time, it becomes difficult to really work on and improve any aspect of your playing. Try focusing on one aspect at a time. In this meditation, we are focusing on the sound. Whatever your instrument, practice playing long tones, so that you don't have to think about rhythms. Allow yourself to be fully absorbed by the sound you are producing.

You can also meditate on creating a big, full, beautiful sound. Listen, relax, breathe, and fill up your space with sound. Imagine yourself in a big hall, and envision yourself playing to a person way up in the last row of the balcony. Fill up the entire hall with sound. Imagine the sound. Imagine the sound filling up the big space. ♟

Many people get nervous in a big hall with lots of people, but if you envision yourself playing in a situation such as this, you have already practiced what it would sound and feel like. As much as you can, try to envision yourself in different performance spaces, as you practice at home or in a practice room. Don't just play to the little room. Imagine and use visualization to fill the space with beautiful music and sound.

COUNTING MEDITATION

The counting meditation is a favorite among many of my students. It is actually one of the easier meditations to practice because we are giving the mind another point of focus. Not only are we focused on the breath, but we are focused on the task of counting numbers. If your mind tends to wander a lot, then this meditation might work well for you.

♟ Counting meditation can be practiced with many variations. Start in a comfortable seated position. Connect with your breath, coming into the basic breath meditation to bring your attention to the present moment. Then, visualize that you are writing a big number 1 right in front of you, as you inhale and exhale slowly. Then, slowly draw a big number 2, as you inhale and exhale. Continue drawing each number: 3, 4, 5, etc., up to 9, as you inhale and exhale for each number. Once you reach 9, then start again at 1. If you happen to lose track of what number you are on, start back at number 1 and continue.

You can vary this meditation by visualizing that you are using different writing utensils. You can draw with a pen, pencil, crayon, marker, etc. I like to paint, so I like to imagine that I have a Chinese paintbrush. ♟

Counting meditation is also excellent if you are having a difficult time falling asleep. To vary this exercise for sleep, practice while you are lying in bed. Connect with a soft breath in and a soft breath out. Visualize the numbers in reverse order, starting with the number 9, 8, 7, 6, etc., all the way down to 1. Once you reach 1, then start again at 9. Counting backwards helps to release the mind so that you can relax even further. If you lose track of what number you are on, simply start again at 9 and continue counting backwards. I guess there is something to counting those sheep after all!

If you try the sleeping meditation and prefer counting backwards instead of forwards, then try the counting meditation counting backwards instead. It really doesn't matter. All that matters is that you stay focused on drawing the numbers and coordinating that with the breath.

COUNTING MEDITATION WITH YOUR INSTRUMENT

The counting meditation can be applied to playing your music by getting into the rhythm and flow of your piece.

🧘 Be fully present in the rhythm of your piece. Make it steady and even. This can help tremendously if you tend to rush through your pieces. Try playing along with a metronome or a play-along track, and keep your body relaxed. Play your scales or musical patterns in an even rhythm, meditating on the evenness of your fingers or hands.

Another application is to coordinate your breath to counting rests. The next time you are playing in an ensemble, counting rests, waiting to play your part or in a band waiting for your time to solo, make sure that you breathe deeply and have a full breath with the rhythm of the music. For example, inhale as you count | 1 2 3 4 | 2 2 3 4 |, and exhale as you count | 3 2 3 4 | 4 2 3 4 |. By counting and breathing in this way, you are practicing a calming breath while you are resting, rather than a shallow breath. As the tempo speeds up, you are more inclined to have a shallow breath, so find a relaxed rhythm with the breath according to the tempo of your piece.

When you count the rests, use your fingers as another source of tactile focus for the mind, similar to counting rosary or mala beads.

This is how meditation and breathing can help you focus and be in the moment. Even when you are resting or waiting to play, you should be in the moment, listening to the music, breathing deeply, and clearing your mind so that you can be present when it's your time to play. 🧘

WALKING MEDITATION

In a walking meditation, we coordinate our steps with our breath. Depending on how fast or slow you are walking, you can vary the rate of your breathing.

The walking meditation can be practiced walking to a performance, walking on stage, walking to class, or just about anywhere you happen to be walking. If you are walking across streets, be very careful and alert! You can get the most benefit out of this meditation if you can find a safe place that you can practice, free from cars, bikes, or other moving things. This is a great one to practice in a park. You also don't need a lot of space, especially if you are walking slowly, so you can also practice inside. Simply connect your breath to your steps.

🧘 Start walking slowly, inhaling as you take two steps and then exhaling as you take two steps. If this doesn't feel quite right, try inhaling to a count of 3 or 4 and exhaling to a count of 3 or 4. When the inhalation and exhalation are the same length, we regulate the breath, making it even. So, we are dealing with even ratios: 2:2, 3:3, 4:4, etc. If your mind gets carried away and you lose track of counting your steps, simply notice that it happened and bring your attention back to counting the steps as you breathe in and out.

If you are stressed and need to calm down even more, make the exhale twice as long as the inhale. For example, try inhaling to a count of two steps and exhaling to a count of four steps, and notice how you feel. Now we are dealing with ratios of 2:4, 3:6, 4:8, etc. Any time you exhale longer than you inhale, the body and the mind feel more relaxed. This is a nice one to practice as you are walking to your gig or walking on stage.

Exhaling is an opportunity to release, relax, and let go of negative thoughts, feelings, emotions, aches and pains, etc. Visualize that you are letting go of anything that you do not need, such as negative thoughts or anything that is no longer serving you. Just let it go.

If you need to become more energized, make the inhales longer than the exhales. Most important is to find a comfortable, relaxed pace that will give you the outcome that you are looking for. 🧘

WALKING MEDITATION: VISUALIZING YOUR MUSIC

The walking meditation can also be used to practice visualizing your music when you don't have your instrument.

♟ Visualize yourself playing your instrument while walking in the same tempo as the piece that you are visualizing. Can you visualize playing your scales and arpeggios with an even tempo? There are many variations to explore, and I would encourage you to find and create various meditations according to what you need to work on.

The natural tendency when playing fast is to hold the breath or tense up the body. The better approach would be to deepen the breath and stay relaxed so that there is more energy left for the music. Visualize yourself playing your music with ease of movement in the body. Imagine yourself being calm and relaxed, yet energized and alert at the same time. Walk with a steady tempo, and stay relaxed. ♟

MEDITATION IN MOTION

The walking meditation is a meditation in motion. Keeping your focus on the breath as you practice yoga and as you practice your instrument are other forms of meditation in motion. Every musical endeavor could be a meditation in motion. You don't have to be still to meditate. You don't even have to "look" like you are meditating. Meditation can happen almost anytime and anywhere. You can meditate on the subway on the way to your gig.

Simply focus on one particular thing and allow the thoughts to come and go, detaching yourself from the mind chatter. Observe the mind, and continually bring your attention back to your focus.

POSTURE MEDITATION

As we have discovered with the previous exercises, practicing your instrument can become a form of meditation. The focus can be on sound, breath, rhythm, repetitive sequences, scales, or chord studies. As you practice, you can also use the focus on your posture as a meditation.

🧘 When you practice, notice how you are holding your instrument. How is your posture? Can you release and let go of any tension, simply by bringing your awareness to the area or areas of the body? Practice observing how it feels to play your instrument while relaxed. Are you bringing in extra tension? How are your shoulders, arms, wrists, and fingers? Are you playing relaxed?

Notice your breath. Are you breathing full and deep, or short and shallow? Begin to deepen the breath. Play your phrases and lines with a steady, even breath.

Allow the rhythm of what you are playing to become a meditation. Be totally present, totally aware, and totally relaxed. Usually, when we start to think or concentrate on any one particular thing—especially if it is something new that we are learning—we lose track of our breath and our posture. Try to keep this awareness of posture and breath as you practice something that is familiar to you, such as scales, arpeggios, long-tone exercises, or drum rudiments. The new way of practicing with good posture and full breaths, playing with ease and freedom of movement, will become more natural and will become your new way of playing with ease. 🧘

Many people get uncomfortable when there is silence. I see this a lot with novice jazz musicians, when they improvise. I can tell that some of my students are not comfortable with the silence, as they want to fill up the space with lots of notes. They don't allow the music to breathe. Enjoy the silence. Make it a part of the music. The music needs space, and so do the listeners' ears. We tend to play more when our minds get cluttered with chatter, just as many people tend to talk more when they get nervous.

I also see this in classical musicians. Take your time with the fermatas and cadenzas. Feel that you have all of the time in the world to play your music, so that you don't rush through your pieces. This is especially helpful to keep in mind when you play difficult passages. Nerves tend to make us rush. Slow down and enjoy the journey. Stay in the present moment. Ride the breath.

A STORY ON PRACTICING BEFORE A CONCERT MEDITATION

One of the most amazing experiences that I have had was when I was on a concert tour with a trio. We were to perform in a church that had been converted into a concert space. Matt, fellow flutist and yoga enthusiast, and I arrived early that day to check out the space and get a feel for the room. Matt and I had always talked about recording an improvised two-flute CD. Once we heard the natural acoustics, we knew that this was the time and space to record our CD. We had the hall for the whole day so that we could prepare for our concert that evening. The result was a CD entitled *Meditations in a Contemporary World*. I was playing flute, and Matt was playing alto flute.

The funny thing is that Matt really didn't feel like doing it at the time, but I said, "How can we pass this opportunity up?" Now is the time. He agreed, so we set up our recording equipment. He called out a mode that we would play in, hit Play, and we started improvising.

We were both totally present and listened to each other and to the sounds around us. You could hear cars in the distance as well as the sound of a distant foghorn. We let all of these sounds in and reacted and incorporated that into our sound meditation. I have never had a more relaxing, energizing warm-up before any concert, as the day we did this recording. When it came time to perform the concert, I felt a real connection with the space and the musicians. The program I chose to perform was mostly classical and very demanding and challenging, but I felt at ease.

We used the afternoon as a meditation to prepare for the concert. We were practicing non-attachment in our performance. We had no preconceived notion as to what we were going to create or how it was going to turn out. We allowed the music to flow through us.

The outcome was one of the best performances I have experienced. We were able to connect with each other in the present moment and tap into the universal consciousness. Our improvisations sounded like they were composed, but free. When people listen to the CD, they think that the music was actually written down and composed beforehand. Some have even asked us for the scores. I believe the reason that it came out so well was because we were totally present and in the moment, being in tune with each other, with our environment, and with all of the sounds that surround us. There was non-attachment to the process of creation and to the outcome.

You never know when you will find that moment. Through practicing meditation, you will be prepared to meet the moment, whenever that may be. You will probably never feel ready.

If Matt had gone with that feeling of "I don't feel like doing this now," it never would have happened. We didn't have any agenda or preconceived idea of how it was going to go or what we were going to do. When we try to control everything, life can get more challenging, because so many things are out of our control. It is important to try and go with the flow, seize the moment, and let go of attachment. When you do, you can rise to the occasion and discover new possibilities and new ways of being.

By practicing meditation, you learn to stay present and go with the flow. If we tried to set it all up beforehand, I am sure the results would have been much different. How often do we feel "totally" prepared to do anything? There may be reservation or hesitation. I have also noticed that in various situations when I feel at my lowest, I actually perform at my best. Sometimes, you just have to go for it.

When we practice meditation, we get in touch with our center. Once you develop this awareness, whenever there is chaos around you, you can be unaffected. You can keep your center and separate yourself from the chaos. You learn that wherever you go and whatever situation you find yourself in, you have this center. You will be able to develop an awareness of this center and have the calmness within, so that you can work under pressure and feel comfortable and centered while you perform. This awareness will enhance and enrich your performance.

You will be able to develop an awareness that you are not your thoughts. You can observe your thoughts and practice non-attachment. No matter what your thoughts or emotions are, let things go. Nothing can touch your center. You can become totally in the moment and perform your best.

The more we practice meditation, the more we can separate ourselves from our mind chatter. If we listen to and accept the mind chatter, we can work ourselves into a frenzy. If we can begin to see this chatter for what it is, we will be able to have more control over our thoughts, as we realize that we do not have to engage in every thought or feeling. Let it drift or float by.

If you develop a daily practice of meditation, it will be so much easier to use the techniques because they will be like familiar friends. They will be there supporting you in difficult times. It's always helpful to have a support system around you. When we practice meditation and visualization, we are developing a support system for ourselves. We all know that it is much easier to do things with a support system.

When you become the witness, you begin to see your mind chatter for what it is. You realize that you are not your thoughts. Practicing meditation teaches us to clear the mind chatter so that we can be in the moment and enjoy our performance. If we start doubting ourselves before or during a performance, what happens is our mind chatter is turned up. It takes us out of the present moment and tries to distract us from our performance. We need to start to find the still, silent, calm space between all of those thoughts. This is our true center. This is the peace within.

Ideas come to us when we are in this state of relaxation. So many ideas come when I am on vacation. You may have had this experience too—when you are relaxing and all of a sudden an idea comes to you. Usually, the harder you try, the more difficult it is. Sometimes, when we try too hard, we get tense, and ideas don't come.

As discussed, there are many different types of meditation. Using them effectively can help you achieve your full potential as a musician. As we all know, the more focus and concentration that we can develop, the more solid and convincing our performances will be. By practicing meditation, we can get to this goal much more quickly. We can also use meditation in combination with visualization to help us along our paths.

VISUALIZATION MEDITATIONS

Visualization can help us achieve a particular outcome, such as playing a particular passage or piece beautifully or flawlessly. We can meditate on a particular goal or outcome as our focus.

If you are practicing visualizing yourself for a performance, you are imagining what it would be like and feel like when you are in that situation, so that you can prepare yourself better. Imagine yourself in front of different audiences and in different rooms. Observe your thoughts, feelings, emotions, and body sensations. Take it all in and see if you can exhale it away and find your center—that space that *is* you.

EXERCISE 1 Room Meditation

♟ Come into a comfortable seated position with the eyes closed or have a soft gaze. Take a few minutes to visualize that you are going on stage to play for an empty room. How would it feel to play for an empty room? Would you like that? What is the mind saying? What is the body feeling? Sit with this sensation for a while, and breathe into the experience. Notice as much as you can about putting yourself into this experience.

Now visualize playing for a full room. You have just come on stage and see a huge room full of people. How would it feel to play for a full room? What thoughts are going through your mind? How does your body feel? Sit with this sensation for a while, and breathe into the experience. Notice as much as you can about putting yourself into this experience.

After spending a few minutes visualizing the empty room and full room, compare your experiences. Which one did you like better? Which one is more comfortable? Some people feel more comfortable playing for no audience. It's usually easier to play better in the practice room scenario. Others would feel disappointed that no one came to see them perform and maybe wonder, doesn't anyone like my music? Some people would feel very uncomfortable playing for such a large crowd. But what if you thought of these situations in another way? If there were no audience, you may have to ask yourself, was there adequate advertising? What other events are happening in town at the same time? Was there inclement weather? It may have nothing to do with you or your musical abilities.

EXERCISE 2 Audition Meditation

Visualize yourself in an audition room. See yourself standing tall and confident. **Mountain pose** (see p. 45) and **warrior** postures (see pp. 83–87), are good to develop this source of strength and confidence. Feel your feet grounding and connecting with the floor beneath you. Feel your deep breath with a long, slow exhale. Visualize your audition team wanting the best for you. Imagine that they want you to do well. You have to think that they want to hear the best in you. Dwell upon the positive, not the negative.

EXERCISE 3   Positive Meditation

If you put things into a different perspective and have a different outlook, maybe your experiences can change for the better. If you get anxious before a large audience, think about it differently. What if you felt honored that all of these people at the concert took the time to come hear you play because they wanted to hear you? Can you imagine that they want you to do well?

Visualize being excited to be there to perform for them and being more relaxed. We get nervous when our mind chatter is vying for our attention, and therefore, we can't concentrate on what we really need to put our energy into: performing and playing our best.

In Kundalini yoga, we sing a blessing at the end of each class. It is, "May the long time sun shine upon you, all love surround you, and the pure light within you, guide your way on." It is a wonderful blessing to keep in mind, through your daily life. What if that was your mantra before you played? If you can find a positive saying that resonates with you, that you can say to yourself before you go on stage, then there will be no fear—only positive energy that will emanate from you as you perform. Connect with that positive feeling before you go on stage. That way there will be only positive thoughts for all.

EXERCISE 4   Finding Your Center

Where is your most comfortable place in this world? It's the place where you feel the most calm, relaxed, and non-judgmental. It could be a place you have actually been to, or it could be a place that you envision in your mind. It could be on your front porch, in your garden, or on a white sandy beach—any place special for you. Try to get all of your senses involved so that your place becomes real. How does your body feel in this place? How does your mind feel in this place?

For example, if your safe place is on a white sandy beach, visualize the blue sky and sea. Feel the warm breeze on your skin, and smell the salty air. Imagine, feel, see, and smell as many details about this place as you can.

For some of us, the concert stage is our safe place. If not, can you imagine it being your safe place and finding your center on stage? Visualize finding your center on the concert stage.

It is important to have a place like this to retreat to, when life gets tough. If you get stressed, you can go there and get relief by envisioning yourself there. Your safe place can also be a nice place to practice your meditation so that when thoughts or experiences arise in your mind, you can step back from them and know that you are safe and protected in your place, and that nobody can get to you physically, mentally, or emotionally. This is your center. No matter where you go, your center or home is always with you. ♟

You can use meditation and visualization as a way to find out what you need to practice. You can visualize yourself in various situations, such as sitting in the green room before a performance, or in an interview or audition, and try to imagine how your thoughts would be. What would be worrisome or bothersome? How would your body feel? What would your breath be like? Then, take whatever comes to mind, and turn it into a positive, such as visualizing yourself being relaxed and comfortable, breathing deeply and freely, playing beautifully and with ease of movement. Being fully present and calm.

If we can shift our perspective and visualize more positive outcomes, this is when we will get results. We are all energetic beings. The energy that we put out will be the energy that we get back. So, if you want a positive outcome, visualize it and meditate on it. The more positive energy we give, the more positive energy we will receive. If you can think more positively, you will probably have a more positive experience. Do you usually see your glass as half empty or half full? If we can start to see our lives and experiences in a more positive light, or from the "glass is half full" perspective, our outlook on life can change dramatically.

Meditation Techniques

Meditations	Benefits	Page
Breath	relaxes the mind	25
Mantra	promotes peace	28
Counting	releases the mind fully	29
Walking Meditation	calms the entire being	31
Meditation in Motion	brings meditation to daily activities	32
Visualization Meditations	helps prepare for specific events	36

CHAPTER 4

Posture and Alignment

In order to build a strong body for your instrument, it is necessary to start with building your foundation, which is good posture and proper body alignment. Each instrument presents its own set of physical challenges. In yoga, we practice paying close attention to how we carry our bodies and how we feel. The awareness you develop by practicing yoga techniques will carry over to how you practice your instrument. You will become more aware of how you hold and carry your body as you practice and as you go about your activities. For example, if you start to feel pain or tension in your body, how can you move or shift your position so that you can make it easier to play? Or, maybe you have been practicing for too long, and you just need to take a few minutes to stretch your body in the opposite way of how you have been holding and playing your instrument.

Many musicians tend to round the shoulders, hunch the back, or lift one shoulder, creating a curve in the spine when they play. These positions are very common for many instrumentalists, as it is the nature of playing some of these instruments. If you keep practicing your instrument in these positions hour after hour, day after day, year after year, you may wind up with back and/or neck problems. If you are aware of being in these positions, you can counteract them by becoming more aware of how you carry or play your instrument, and you can practice exercises to teach the spine another way of being.

Rounding the back is one of the most common issues I see in musicians. Let's see how simple awareness can change how we hold ourselves. There are many exercises you can do to counteract this rounding of the back, which I will share with you. But first, let's try a simple exercise to see how it feels. You can practice this one at anytime throughout the day to bring more awareness to your posture.

YOGA MUDRA EXERCISE

🧘 Draw your shoulders back and down. Imagine that the shoulder blades could touch each other. They won't, of course, but having this visualization of the direction we are heading towards with the shoulders will show you how to open the front of the body and chest area and relax the shoulders at the same time. Another way to practice this opening is to clasp your hands behind your back, drawing your hands behind you to open the front of your body. This is called the **yoga mudra** hand position. This is a great exercise to do frequently throughout the day. It relieves stress in the shoulder area and also opens the front of the body. 🧘

Many of the yoga exercises will help you become more aware of your spinal alignment and your breath. You will then be able to bring this awareness to how you practice your instrument. Once you become aware, it is hard not to notice.

A student once told me that he was overwhelmed by all of the information his body was giving him, once he started listening and paying attention. He had no idea that he was going through life with such little awareness. Once he started practicing and shifting the way he was doing things, he was amazed to find out how much better he was feeling and how much at ease he was with his playing.

Another student told me that when he went back home for the break between semesters, his mother and many of his friends commented on how much taller he looked. He said it wasn't that he grew any taller, it was just that he was holding himself up straight for the first time. I also noticed this shift in him, and it was exciting to see how his awareness was growing and the progress that he was making.

POSTURE AND MOOD EXERCISE

🧘 In addition to playing with more awareness of posture, a simple shift in posture can also shift our mood. Take a moment to slouch, and notice how you feel. How does the body feel? How is your mood? Put a frown on your face. Pause and notice... how do you feel now?

Now, sit up straight, elongate through your spine, draw your shoulders back and down, and turn up the corners of your mouth just slightly. How does your body feel? How is your mood? Pause and notice...how do you feel now? ♟

Some of my flute students have come to me with a small, thin sound. When I bring their attention to their posture and how they are standing, and give them a few pointers in how to shift it, their sound immediately opens up. This is true for all instruments. If you are slouching or leaning more to one side and are not rooted, all of this can have an effect on your sound production.

It is important to get a firm stance and root through the bottoms of your feet. Even if you are sitting on a chair, keep your feet firmly planted on the ground, hip-width apart and root through your sitting bones. Once you find this position, play from this center.

Having a straight spine allows room for the breath. If you are slouched, you cut off the air stream. If you root through the bottoms of your feet, elongate your spine, lift from the crown of your head, and relax your shoulders back and down to open up your rib cage, you are off to a great start.

This strong foundation of your body will help you produce a good sound, whether you are playing from a standing or seated position, and whether you are an instrumentalist or a vocalist.

When I teach piano, I notice how my students are producing the sound and how their posture is while they are playing. Many people tend to sit too close to the piano. I have them pull the bench a little further away from the piano and sit towards the edge of the bench, rooting through their feet and sitting bones. Then, I make sure that their shoulders are relaxed and that they are also breathing. Many times, instrumentalists that don't have to use their breath to produce the sound on their instrument think that breathing is not that important. Nothing could be further from the truth, as you have experienced in the previous chapter. Whether you are a vocalist, wind player, string player, keyboard player, guitarist, bassist, or drummer, no matter what instrument you play, the breath is important for the music, phrasing, and tone production.

When we are learning something new, we tend to concentrate so hard that we build tension in our bodies, especially in the neck and shoulder areas. Always practice a new technique on music that you feel comfortable with, so you can allow that to be on automatic pilot while you concentrate on your new technique. Keep the breath flowing at all times, and keep relaxing through the body. If you find yourself getting tense, stop, notice, relax, and try again. Whatever you do, don't keep going and letting the tension build more. Keep your awareness.

As you begin to practice your yoga stretches and your instrument with more awareness, take little breaks, and start to become aware of how it feels to play with ease. Whenever you are learning something new, you are trading an old habit for a new habit. You will be teaching your body how to play with proper alignment and ease, as opposed to tension and strain. When you become more aware of your spinal alignment as you practice the yoga techniques, you can take that awareness and feeling back to your practice and remind yourself how proper posture feels when you are playing your instrument or when you go about your daily activities.

A straight spine with relaxed shoulders, arms, wrists, and hands will allow the energy to move freely in the body, which we will be learning in our first pose, **mountain pose**. Practicing with relaxation will allow for more energy for the music.

I was teaching flute lessons to a saxophone doubler, and whenever he became really involved in the flow of the music, his left shoulder would start to build up tension and shrug up towards his ear. When I asked him if he realized that this was happening with his shoulder, he said that he didn't. To remedy this, I told him to play a piece that he was familiar with and to concentrate on relaxing that shoulder as he played. He was able to bring his awareness to this shoulder and play with a relaxed shoulder through most of the piece, but then it started shrugging back up again. When I asked him how that experience felt, he said that he felt that he was much more relaxed for most of it, and that the sound was also much better until he started bringing back the tension at the end. He could start to feel his shoulder shrugging and was aware of what was happening for the first time. When he shifted his awareness to relaxing and letting go of that shoulder, he was able to have more energy for sound production.

He was astounded at how much better his sound was. I had him play the piece a few times so that he could stay relaxed throughout the entire piece. I also said that he would have to be aware of this new way of playing every time he picked up his instrument.

If you lose your newfound awareness, you will go back to your old habits. You will have to practice this new awareness for quite some time until it becomes so natural that it will become your new habit and way of playing. I am always amazed to see what a little shift of awareness can do and how dramatic the effects can be.

MOUNTAIN POSE

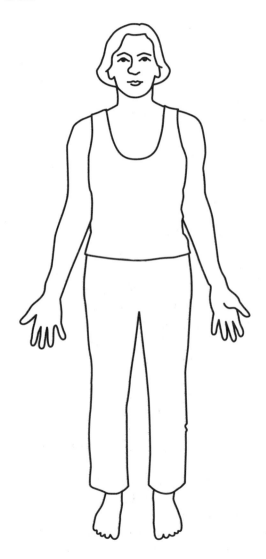

We will take an in-depth look at our fundamental posture for alignment, which is **mountain pose** (*tadasana*, in Sanskrit). **Mountain pose** is the foundation posture for all of the other yoga postures. In this pose, we will learn about proper alignment of the body. Your mother told you to sit up straight for a reason! Proper alignment will allow room for a full breath. It will allow all of the internal organs to be properly aligned and open, and it will allow the body to move freely and with ease. We will carry the alignment principles of **mountain pose** into all of the other yoga poses, as we play our instruments and as we carry our bodies throughout our daily activities.

♟ To practice **mountain pose**, come into a standing position with your feet hip-width apart, feet pointing straight ahead and parallel. Lift and spread the toes nice and wide apart, from the little toe to the big toe. Relax the grip of the toes. Feel the feet spread out, and feel the whole bottoms of the feet in contact with the floor beneath you. Shift your weight slightly forward and back, and from side to side. Notice where you feel your center. Come to a still point to where you feel balanced and centered, grounding through the entire bottoms of the feet. Keep a slight bend in the knees as you engage the muscles of the legs. Never lock any of the joints. Tuck the tailbone just slightly as well, making the pelvis flat as you slightly engage the muscles of the abdomen.

Continue the alignment by drawing the shoulders back and down so that the chest lifts slightly. An easy way to get this feeling is when your arms are down by your side, and you rotate the palms so that they face forward. This automatically opens the shoulders and the chest. Lift from the crown of your head, keeping your chin parallel to the floor. Keep the ears in alignment with the shoulders. This may mean that you have to draw the head back slightly. Lift from the crown of the head. Elongate through the entire spine. You can visualize a helium balloon or a string attached to the crown of your head, elongating and creating space between each vertebrae. Ground through the bottoms of the feet, and lift through the crown of the head.

Once you have all the points of alignment, bring some softness to your posture. Notice if you are trying too hard, and back away slightly. Have the feeling that you are in alignment but that you can move and flow freely without feeling like you are rigid or stiff. Stand in this posture for several breaths.

When you are comfortable with this alignment, try walking slowly with this posture as you breathe the **full yogic breath.** ▲

Another way to think about the alignment is to make sure that the knees are in alignment with the ankles, the hips are in alignment with the knees, the shoulders are stacked above the hips, and the ears stacked above the shoulders. As you elongate with the spine, connect with your **full yogic breath**.

Standing in **mountain pose** allows for ease of movement and gives maximum space for the breath. If you hunch and round the back, caving the chest in, you cannot take a full, deep breath. In **mountain pose**, you can also imagine that you are breathing from the ground up to the sky and from the sky down to the ground. Feel a long line of energy flowing through you from below and from above.

PUT IT INTO PRACTICE

EXERCISE 1   Posture

▲ Yoga develops awareness. Try simple awareness of your posture, to begin. For one week, pay particular attention to how you carry your body. Notice your spinal alignment when you are sitting, standing, and playing your instrument.

How are you carrying your instrument to the gig? Be aware of your posture and how you could make it better. I used to have a shoulder bag, but switched to a backpack, as it was more balanced on both shoulders. How can you carry your instrument with ease? This will have an impact on your playing. By the time you get to the gig, you could be all out of alignment. Be mindful.

Notice if you are carrying any tension in your neck, shoulders, arms, or hands. If you are, shift your posture so that you can be at ease in your body. If you are carrying tension, soften it simply by bringing your attention to it, and exhale it away, letting the tension go with each exhale.

If you learn awareness, and listen to your body, you will also be able to prevent overuse symptoms. If you learn to communicate with your own body and honor what you discover, you can better communicate with others around you and become more aware and present in all that you do.

EXERCISE 2 Breath

Notice the quality of your breath for one week. Whenever you remember, pause and notice how you are breathing. Bring your awareness to the breath and begin to deepen the breath, coming into the **full yogic breath**.

EXERCISE 3 Mindfulness While Playing

Be mindful of everything you do, from the time you put your instrument together until the time you put it back in your case. Notice how you approach your instrument. Are you relaxed? How do you put your instrument together? Move with ease and alignment. How do you pick your instrument up and hold it? Notice how your posture is when you play. Notice how your breath is when you play. Be the observer all of the time. If there is anything that feels uncomfortable, shift so that you can play with ease.

You can practice awareness of posture and breath at any time or in any place. A prime opportunity for practice is when you are standing in line. How many people like standing in line? Usually, you feel frustrated and would rather not wait. If you shift your perception and use it as an opportunity for practicing breath and posture awareness, your attitude can change dramatically. Instead of slouching and seething, try standing tall and relaxed, then connect with a deep, full breath, and meditate on the breath. You might enjoy standing in line more often and even look for that opportunity to practice.

PRACTICE FOR PERFORMANCE

"I started to combine proper breathing and meditating with more yoga-based stretches whenever I needed to refresh myself after some hours of musical practice and exercises. The result has been surprisingly and radically different. It feels more like replenishing my energy than just refreshing it, allowing me

to concentrate better after longer practice hours, and I get less exhausted at the end of the day."

Many people practice their instrument simply for the sake of practicing, but we should be practicing for performance. So often, I hear students saying after a performance, "I don't know why I didn't play that well. I usually get it right when I play it in the practice room." How often do you perform better in front of an audience than when you practice for yourself? When we play for ourselves, we usually don't have the normal distractions or thoughts that come with a performance.

If you actually visualize yourself in the performance while you are in the practice room, performing becomes so much easier. Visualization is an important tool to use when you practice.

PUT IT INTO PRACTICE

♟ Imagine that you are sitting outside of an audition room waiting for your audition. Take a few moments to observe what is happening in this situation. Ask yourself these questions, and take some time to really notice what is happening in your body and mind. Think about each of the following questions.

What thoughts are running through your mind?

Are you noticing any stress or tension in your muscles?

How does your stomach feel?

How do your shoulders and hands feel?

What is happening with your breath?

Are you speaking with others, or are you by yourself and quiet?

If you are honest with yourself and really pay attention to what came up with this experience, and if there was anything that wasn't pleasant or anything you would like to change, you can practice this same exercise, visualizing how it would feel if you could feel any way you wanted. ♟

The first line of defense is simple breath awareness. We can help ground ourselves in the present moment and help focus our mind with a deep breath in and a long, slow exhale. The exhale is the key element to remember if stress appears. Let the breath be long and slow.

You can practice visualizing yourself in any situation before it happens, and visualize what kind of outcome you would like to have. That way, when you get in that situation, you will have practiced many times what you would like the outcome to be, and you will have prepared yourself for success. This can become one of the most important tools to have in your toolbox for life.

When you practice yoga, think of bringing this experience with you to your performance. You will feel much more grounded, prepared, and confident. You will learn how to get in touch with the center of your being when you practice yoga and be able to bring your center with you wherever you go and with whatever you do. Your center is you, and is unchanged no matter what is going on around you. Whatever distractions, thoughts, or feelings come, you can stay centered, and this is how you build a successful performance. As you learn to get in touch with your center through meditation and observing your thoughts, you can let go of past or future thoughts and distractions and be in the present moment. If you have never been in touch with your center, you will not know how it is supposed to feel to be grounded. Where do you feel your center now?

If we want to immediately center ourselves and be in the present moment, simply bring awareness to your breath. A deep exhale with a sigh can immediately bring you to the present moment, and the sigh will also help relieve stress. Practicing a few of these sighs can also help bring you to your center and make you feel more grounded. If you want to come more fully into the present moment, consciously start to deepen your breath. Doing so will immediately bring your attention to the present moment and relax your mind and body.

In addition to the breath, notice your spinal alignment. If you are slouched or leaning to one side, you are blocking your energy, and you will start to feel like your posture. When you sit or stand tall, you allow your energy to move freely and can feel more at ease.

When you are in the practice room, it can be much easier to put all of your energy into the music. When you get to the performance, there are so many distractions that you are not used to and haven't even thought about, that sometimes you can't give the music your full attention and concentration. It is important to visualize how it will be when you perform, realizing that there will probably be many distractions that will try to carry your mind away from your performance. If you practice imagining what those distractions might be, you can allow them to be there, release them, and stay present with your performance.

Performing in different situations can bring on different feelings and different distractions. If you are performing for people who you know and who are supportive, you will probably be more comfortable than when you are performing for an audition, or any time you are being judged or graded. If you practice for a particular situation, you will actually be able to lessen your anxiety and doubts, as you are preparing yourself and visualizing yourself in this situation so that when you get there, you will have prepared your mind and body for a positive, enjoyable outcome. Practicing yoga with your instrument will develop your awareness and mindfulness and allow you to play with ease and enjoyment.

PUT IT INTO PRACTICE

Here is a checklist of things to be mindful about while you are practicing.

- ♟ While you are playing your instrument, connect with your posture. Think about the alignment in **mountain pose**, and bring that to playing your instrument. Imagine playing from the bottoms of your feet, feeling grounded.

- ♟ Connect with your **full yogic breath** before you play your instrument. Keep this full breath as you play.

- ♟ Bring your awareness to staying relaxed throughout your body when you play your instrument. Make sure your shoulders are relaxed. Relax your arms, wrists, hands, and fingers.

- ♟ Visualize playing a difficult passage with ease. Visualize yourself playing it perfectly and having all of the time in the world to play it.

- ♟ When you are at a rehearsal, practice communicating with your fellow musicians as if you are playing for a performance, so that when you get to the performance, you will be comfortable communicating with your body language.

The applications are endless. Find ways that you can bring more awareness to your playing.

PREVENTING OVERUSE INJURIES THROUGH DEVELOPING THE MIND-BODY CONNECTION

Many musicians develop overuse symptoms. If you play your instrument many hours a day for many years with poor posture or wrong hand position, overuse injuries may develop. Developing the mind-body connection will help prevent overuse injuries and help cure them if they are present. Overuse symptoms are a common problem with musicians, especially in the upper body with the use of hands, wrists, arms, and shoulders. By becoming more aware of your body and breath, you can prevent overuse injuries or even eliminate them all together.

Practicing yoga and meditation will connect your mind and body so that you will become more aware of how you are holding your body and how your mind can affect your body as well. By using the full breath and alignment, the following exercises can help strengthen the mind-body awareness and help prevent or even eliminate these overuse symptoms.

Yoga develops awareness. Begin with practicing awareness of your posture and/or breath. For one week, notice how you carry your body. I give this exercise to my students in the first week of class. We learn about the full, deep breath and proper posture. Then I ask them to practice awareness of their breath and posture for a week. It is so interesting to hear their observations afterwards. One student said, "I noticed how much I was slouching when I played, and once I realized that I was doing it, I changed my posture so that I now sit more upright." He said he was amazed at how much easier it was to play.

If you learn awareness and listen to your body, you will be able to prevent overuse symptoms. If you learn to communicate with your own body, you will better communicate with others around you and become more aware.

PUT IT INTO PRACTICE

🧘 You can try this exercise with many poses, such as **mountain pose** with the arms overhead, or holding the arms out to the side of your body.

Start by coming into **mountain pose.** Inhale your arms up and out to the sides at shoulder height, and press the palms away from you, fingers pointing up to the ceiling. Come into your long, slow, deep breathing, and consciously relax the shoulders. Continue holding this pose for several minutes as you concentrate on the breath. Notice all of the thoughts that come and go as you are holding the pose. Bring your attention back to the breath each time a thought tries to carry you away. Be the observer. Notice what is happening in the mind.

As sensations arise, ask yourself, "Do I really need to come out of the posture when I am tired or can I hold for a little longer? Is my mind telling me that I cannot continue holding the posture, or is it actually my body telling me to stop? See if you can continue to breathe and hold the posture past the first point of urgency to release. If we can hold past that first point of panic or fear, we find that we can become free and light and that we can hold for much-longer than we thought. We learn that our minds can often hold us back from our true potential. If we can detach ourselves from the mind chatter, we can find that we can come closer to our true potential in many aspects of our lives. 🧘

When we release ourselves from constant judgment, we come closer to our true potential. We tend to judge all of our experiences as good or bad. Can you just allow them to be experiences without putting them into one of these categories?

If I keep telling myself that I cannot do a certain thing, will I ever be able to do it? What is the mind chatter telling you time after time? It becomes a daily practice of being mindful of the choices we make and having compassion with ourselves if we get off track. We have the power to channel the chatter into a positive experience.

When we practice being the observer, we learn to develop peace and compassion. We don't attach ourselves to these thoughts or feelings. When we practice yoga, we practice becoming present in all that we do, and we practice how to release judgment.

YOGA OFF THE MAT

"Yoga off the mat" is the process of bringing the knowledge we gain in yoga practice into our daily lives. We bring consciousness and awareness to our choices and our actions.

We don't always need to have a particular routine to practice, but doing so can make "yoga off the mat" easier. The more we learn about how we treat ourselves and what our thoughts are as we practice challenging poses, the more we can learn to observe our thoughts and actions when challenges come into our lives.

You don't have to feel like you have to spend more time doing yet another activity to fill your already full schedule. Find ways to integrate yoga into what you already do, or change other habits such as watching TV to practicing yoga. Notice if you feel different.

We can integrate yoga into our daily lives in so many situations: meditating while you are walking, eating, practicing your instrument, or riding on the subway or bus. You can practice noticing your posture and breath while waiting in line, take relaxing breaths if you get anxious while flying, or exhale with a long sigh anytime you feel on edge. You can be creative in developing your own poses. You can even practice your balance by putting on your socks and shoes while standing on one leg at a time. The list is endless. You can integrate many of the meditations, breath awareness exercises, posture alignment exercises, poses, and stretches at so many points in your day.

Try to practice being mindful in everything you do. So often, we multitask. Try doing just one activity, and really bring your attention to that activity, such as brushing your teeth or eating slowly, really chewing your food and savoring the flavor. You can find so many opportunities throughout your day with the activities that you already do, to be mindful and aware of how you do these activities, both paying attention to the mind and to the physical aspect.

It is important to develop a regular practice routine so that when those really difficult situations arise, you will already be comfortable with the routines.

CHAPTER 5

Upper Body Exercises

"A lot of these exercises are perfect for building strength and stamina in the muscles used in performing. I have had wrist problems for quite some time now, and since I've been keeping up with the exercises, they have been dramatically reduced."

The upper body is the area where most musicians have issues. If we get anxious, we tend to draw our shoulders up to our ears. What we really should be doing is relaxing them back and down, opening up the chest area, and connecting with a long, slow breath. Sometimes, we go around all day not even noticing the tension that we carry in our bodies.

As we go through the various parts of the upper body, we will learn to use tension and release exercises to help us really connect with how it feels to be fully tense and how it feels to be fully relaxed. If we exaggerate the tension, we will really notice how it feels. Then we can consciously release it, relax it, and let it go. This is what is called "tension and release."

The following exercises will help reduce tension and bring strength and flexibility in the upper back, neck, shoulders, arms, wrists, hands, and fingers.

FINGER EXERCISES

♟ Squeeze your fingers together, making fists with both hands. Release the fingers, spreading them wide apart and exhale with a deep "HAA" breath through the mouth. Repeat several times. Then, slowly bend one finger at a time toward the center of the palm to loosen up the fingers. Repeat several times.

Keep the fingers wide open, as you rotate the wrists in one direction several times. Then rotate the wrists in the other direction several times.

LION POSE

The **lion pose** also works very well with the finger exercises and will help energize the muscles of the whole face as well as the hands. To add the **lion pose**, take a breath in as you close the eyes, scrunch up all of the muscles in the face, hold the breath, and make fists with the hands. To release, exhale with a big "HAA" or roar, and open the hands, spreading the fingers wide, and open the eyes wide, looking up as you stick the tongue way out, reaching towards the chin. This will stretch out all the muscles of the face and hands. Producing sound is also a great way to release tension in the body.

HAND EXERCISES

Hold the right hand in front of your body, with the elbow straight, like you were telling someone to stop. Take your left hand, and press all the fingers of the right hand (including the thumb) towards you, stretching the under part of the arm and the wrist. Relax your neck and shoulders, and breathe. Hold for a few breaths, then release the stretch and shake it out.

Now, hold the right hand in front of your body with the elbow straight, and allow the wrist to bend, pointing the fingers down. Gently draw the back of the right hand and fingers towards you with your left hand, stretching the top part of your arm. Relax your neck and shoulders, and breathe. Shake it out, and repeat the same sequence with the other hand.

Hand Variations

You can also draw the four fingers back towards you and then the thumb by itself or draw one finger at a time back towards you. Shake it out, and change hands.

Another variation for the fingers is to draw one finger at a time towards the center of the palms to stretch the fingers in the opposite direction.

As you practice these hand variations, make sure that you keep the shoulders relaxed. If you notice that they are getting tense, use a **tension/release** exercise as described in the exercise "Shoulders: Tension and Release," to make sure that your shoulders are really relaxed while you stretch out the arms and wrists.

WRIST AND ARM ROTATIONS

With the elbows bent, rotate the wrists away from each other in circles. As you do this, feel free to move the fingers creatively, loosening them up. Then, rotate the wrists towards each other in circles. Pause, then rotate the forearms and hands towards each other in a circle in front of the body. Then rotate them away from each other.

SHOULDERS: TENSION AND RELEASE

Inhale as you draw the shoulders up to your ears. Squeeze the shoulders up as high as you can, holding the breath in. Exhale with a sigh, as you drop and release the shoulders. Relax, and repeat two more times.

You can use the concept of tension and release in many ways. If at any time you are not sure that your muscles are fully relaxed, consciously exaggerate the tension, then let it go.

SHOULDER CIRCLES

Inhale the shoulders up towards your ears, then exhale, rotating the shoulders back and down, opening up the chest area. As your shoulders come all the way down, inhale the shoulders forward, rounding the back, and continue the rotation until the shoulders come all the way up to your ears again. Continue with the shoulder rotations, making full circles.

Reverse directions, exhaling the shoulders forward and down, rounding the back of the body. As the shoulders come all the way down, start to inhale the shoulders back, opening up the chest area, then up to your ears once again. Continue with shoulder rotations, making full circles coming forward.

Shoulder Variations

As a variation, you can circle one shoulder, then the other. For another variation, you can bend the elbows, resting the fingers on top of the shoulders as you circle the elbows in one direction and then the other.

NECK CIRCLES: HALF AND FULL

Come into a standing or seated position with your spine tall, shoulders relaxed. Connect with your deep breath. On an exhale, allow the chin to rest towards your chest. Imagine that you are taking the breath into the back of your neck to release, and melt away any tension. Keep the chin down as you inhale your chin to your right shoulder, and breathe into the left side of the neck. Exhale your chin towards your chest, and inhale your chin to your left shoulder, breathing into the right side of the neck. Continue with half circles in front of the body. Then, come into full circles, being gentle as the head comes back. Inhale as the head comes to one side and back, and exhale as the head goes to the other side and down. Reverse directions.

Neck Variations

Instead of drawing the chin to either side, you can draw the ears to either side to feel a slightly different stretch in the neck. Keeping the chin parallel to the ground, inhale at center, and as you exhale, draw the right ear towards the right shoulder. Relax the left shoulder and breathe into the left side of the neck for a few deep breaths. Imagine that you are taking the breath to any point of sensation or tension you may find in the neck, and allow the tension to melt away on the exhale. Slowly inhale the head back to center. Pause at center for a moment, noticing the difference between the two sides. Repeat the same sequence on the other side, exhaling the left ear towards the left shoulder. After you slowly inhale the head back to center, pause and notice the effects of this stretch.

SHOULDER STRETCH

Draw your right arm across your chest using your left arm to hug it into your chest, giving a stretch between the shoulder blades.

Keep the shoulders relaxed. Take several long, slow breaths in this position. You can also experiment with making some movements with the head, drawing your left ear towards your left shoulder. This will help release the right neck and shoulder at the same time. When you are ready to release, draw the head back to center, release the arms, and wiggle it out. Pause to notice the difference between how the two sides feel. Repeat the same sequence on the other side.

TRICEP STRETCH

With your right arm, pat yourself on the right side of your back. With your left hand, draw your right elbow back more, feeling a nice stretch on the underside of your arm. Pause here for several breaths. Take your breath to the place where you feel the stretch, and use the exhale to melt away tension. Move into **cow face arms**, or release this stretch and repeat on the other side.

COW FACE ARMS

As a variation to the tricep stretch, you can move into **cow face arms**. With your right arm, pat yourself on the back, drawing your hand towards the center of your back. With your left arm, reach behind your back, drawing it up the center of your back. Try to clasp your hands behind your back. Breathe here for several breaths, then release and repeat on the other side.

If you cannot reach to clasp your hands in this position, you can grab a belt or towel and work towards bringing your hands together over time. 🧘

EAGLE ARMS

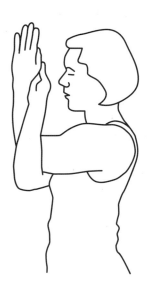

"By exercising my body with yoga weekly and also daily, it changed my life cycle deeply. The main usage of yoga is when I practice my piano. I usually perform a few yoga positions before I start practicing. One of my favorite positions is eagle arms, where you cross your arm and stretch out your arm muscles."

Eagle arms is one of the best exercises to stretch the place between the shoulder blades. If you cannot come into the full **eagle arms** with the palms touching right away, you can try grabbing onto one finger, or keep the palms facing away from each other. Find an arm position where you can feel a good stretch between the shoulder blades. If this position does not work for you, then stay with the **shoulder stretch**. Many people find **eagle arms** difficult at first. It is not important if you can do the posture or not. It is important that you find a stretch that works well for your body.

♟ To come into **eagle arms**, inhale as you extend your arms out to the side in a T position with your palms facing down. Exhale the arms in front of you with the right arm under the left arm, crossing at the elbows. Try to get the top elbow over a little further than the bottom elbow, if you can. Bend the elbows so that the palms face away from each other. Draw the right hand towards your nose, and wrap it around the left hand so that the palms are touching and fingers are pointing up towards the sky. If you can't clasp the palms together fully, go to a point where you can feel the stretch between the shoulders. You may even be able to grab a finger. Breathe into the back of the body, opening the space between the shoulders. Pause here for several breaths. Move directly into **eagle arms variations** or release this side slowly, and repeat the sequence on the other side.

Eagle Arms Variations

In **eagle arms** position, inhale as you draw the elbows up, and exhale as you draw the elbows down, to feel the stretch in different places. Rotate the elbows in circles in one direction, coordinating the breath with the movement, then in the other direction to loosen them up more. Bring them back to center, and slowly release the arms. Shake or wiggle it out, notice the difference between the two sides, then repeat the whole sequence on the other side. ♟

STANDING YOGA MUDRA

Yoga mudra hand position is one of the best stretches to open up the front of the body and teach your shoulders to draw back. It is a wonderful stretch to do throughout the day whenever you feel you need to release the upper back and shoulders. It is also a nice counter-stretch to **eagle arms**.

♟ Start with your feet a little wider than hip-width apart, toes pointing parallel to each other. Keep a slight bend in the knees. Inhale the arms straight up in front of you. Exhale, drawing them back behind the body, clasping the hands together in the **yoga mudra** hand position. Elongate the spine, lifting the crown of your head. Inhale as you draw the hands up towards the ceiling and

exhale, drawing them back down towards the floor. Do this a few times to loosen up the upper body.

To come into the full posture, inhale, and then as you exhale, lead with your chest as you come into a **forward bend** (see p. 74). Make sure to keep the knees slightly bent to protect the lower back. If it is uncomfortable for the head to come so low in a complete **forward bend**, you can try coming halfway down. Allow the head to fully relax. You may want to gently move your head from side to side and forward and back. Move your head, as you would shake it when you say "yes" and "no," a few times slowly to make sure it is fully relaxed. The arms continue to reach up toward the ceiling and down towards the floor.

You can make micro movements with the arms, moving slightly from side to side, and notice how the stretch changes. If the arms get tired, you can keep the hands clasped, bend the elbows to release for a few breaths, then straighten the arms. You may find that the hands can go even further after the release. Continue to draw the arms up and back, feeling a nice stretch in the shoulders for a few more breaths.

To release from the stretch, bend the knees a little deeper. Press through the soles of the feet, and let that press slowly lift you back to standing. Take at least three breaths to bring you back to standing. Once you reach standing position, allow the hands to release as the arms float back to your sides. Pause here, and notice how you feel. ♟

In any inversion, such as forward bends, or any time the head is below the heart, always come out of the posture very slowly. Otherwise, you may get dizzy. Moving slowly out of the inversion will help regulate the blood flow.

HELICOPTER

Helicopter is one of the best exercises to release tension in the upper body. This movement can be practiced with the breath, as described in chapter 2, or by itself, as described here.

♟ Stand with the feet a little wider than hip-width apart. Relax your arms down by your side, then start turning your torso from side to side. As you turn from side to side, look over each shoulder, bringing the twist from the base of the spine all the way to the crown of the head. Really allow the arms to be loose and relaxed, allowing them to flop back and forth. The arms should be so relaxed that they simply flop from side to side, hitting whatever part of the body they may land, as the torso moves from side to side. Keep the corners of your mouth turned up slightly, and notice how that can also shift your mood. When you are ready to release, release the movement slowly, finding your way back to center. Pause and notice how the upper body feels. ♟

PUT IT INTO PRACTICE

♟ Here is an exercise routine for the upper body. Start in **mountain pose** with the following centering meditation. Close your eyes or have a soft gaze. Bring your attention to the present moment by noticing the sounds around you. Notice the sounds in the room, then notice the sounds outside the room. Allow your ear to jump from sound to sound. Resist the urge to identify the sounds or their source.

Release these sounds, and bring your attention to your body, standing on the floor. Notice what is touching the floor. Then scan your body, and notice whether you are holding tension. If you are, simply bring your attention to this area or areas in the body, and begin to release the tension. Then notice the breath, without trying to change it, at first. Notice the quality of the breath. Is it long or short? Is it deep or shallow? Now that you have awareness of the breath, begin to expand it.

Come into the **full yogic breath** gradually. Each time you exhale, exhale a little more; each time you inhale, inhale a little more. As you exhale, draw the muscles of your abdomen in and up towards the spine. As you inhale, relax these muscles and allow the air to flow in freely. Feel the expansion of breath in the whole rib cage area, expanding the front, back, and sides of the body. Imagine the whole rib cage area is like a balloon, expanding in all directions as you inhale and contracting as you exhale.

After you have connected with this full breath, release your chin towards your chest. Try not to collapse into the chest, but feel the chest and top of the neck lifting slightly. Imagine that each exhale is an opportunity to release and let go of any tension that may be found in the body. Each inhale is an opportunity to gather anything you may need, such as energy or a positive outlook.

On the next breath in, draw the chin back to center. As you exhale, draw the ear or chin towards your right shoulder. Inhale on this side, and as you exhale, draw the chin towards your chest. Inhale the ear or chin to the left side. Exhale the chin back to center, and continue **half neck circles** from side to side for a few times, coordinating the breath with the movement.

From the **half neck circles**, you can come into **full neck circles**, if that is comfortable for the neck. Be gentle as the head goes back, coordinating the breath with the movement. Inhale as the head comes to one side and back, exhale as the head goes to the other side and down. Circle a few times slowly in one direction, and repeat the same number of times in the other direction. Notice any sounds or sensations in the neck area. If you find any areas of tightness as you are exploring your circles, feel free to roam around in that area or areas, releasing any tension by pausing and breathing into that sensation. Allow the exhale to melt the tension away.

Bring the head back up to center, and move into **shoulder circles**. Inhale, round the shoulders, then draw them up to your ears. Exhale as you draw them back and down. Keep the breath flowing as you move through the circles. Reverse the direction of the circles. Release and notice.

Move into the **hand exercises** by extending your right hand forward as if you were going to tell someone to stop. Draw the fingers towards you with your other hand stretching the wrist and under part of the arm. Notice the right shoulder. Squeeze it up to your ear, and relax it down. Hold for a few deep breaths, then draw the fingertips down, drawing the back of the hand and fingers towards you with the other hand. Hold for a few breaths, as you stretch the upper part of the wrist and arm. Release and shake the hand out. Repeat the same sequence with the left hand.

With the arms in a comfortable position, take both hands and spread the fingers wide apart. Start with the thumbs and draw one finger at a time towards the center of the palm. Do this a few times, then keep the fingers spread wide apart as you rotate the wrists in one direction, then the other direction. Release the wrists, and circle from the elbow. Reverse directions. Circle from the shoulders by placing the hands lightly on the shoulders for a more supportive stretch, or make full circles with the arms. Reverse directions. Shake it all out, and let it go with a sigh.

Come into a **shoulder stretch** by drawing your right arm across the front of your body, and hold it in close to your chest with the left hand. Relax the right shoulder, and feel the stretch across the upper back and right shoulder. Hold for a few deep breaths, and release from this stretch. Draw the right arm back like you were going to pat yourself on your back, coming into the **tricep stretch**. Draw the right elbow back with your left hand. Pause here for several breaths. Release the stretch or come into **cow face arms** by bending your left elbow and drawing it behind your back to clasp your hands together. Take several breaths, breathing into the sensation. When you are ready to release, release slowly and wiggle or shake it out. Pause and notice the difference between the right and left side. Repeat the same sequence on the other side. Remember to take a few deep, relaxed breaths into each one of your stretches and each one of your poses.

Come into **eagle arms**. When you cross your arms, it is helpful if you can get the top elbow over a little further than the bottom elbow. Feel the stretch between the shoulder blades. Even if you can't clasp your hands, it's okay. Inhale your arms up towards the ceiling, and exhale your elbows down towards the ground. Move your elbows from side to side. Circle your elbows in one direction, coordinating the breath with the movement, then into the other direction. Breathe into the sensation, allowing the exhales to release and let go. Then bring your arms back to center.

Keep the eagle arm position with the hands by your forehead. Inhale, then as you exhale, bend your knees, bringing the elbows towards the knees as you come into a **forward bend**. Inhale, and as you exhale, slowly bring the hands towards the ground. They will probably not touch the ground. Only go as far as you feel a nice stretch. Make sure to fully release the head, relaxing the chin towards the chest. Pause here for several breaths, as you breathe into the space between the shoulder blades. When you are ready to come out, slowly draw the hands back towards your forehead. Bend the knees a little deeper. Press into the bottoms of the feet, and let that press slowly bring you back up to standing position.

Always come up very slowly from **forward bend**s. Remember that any time your head is below the heart, it is important to move slowly to regulate the blood flow. Slowly release the arms, shake it out, and exhale it away with a sigh. Pause and notice how the upper body feels. Repeat the **eagle arms** sequence on the other side.

To release the upper body stretches, come into the **helicopter**. Stand with the feet a little wider than hip-width apart. Allow the arms to relax down by your side, then start turning your torso from side to side. As you turn from side to side, look over each shoulder, bringing the twist from the base of the spine all the way to the crown of the head. Really allow the arms to relax and flop back and forth. The arms should be so relaxed that they simply flop from side to side, hitting whatever part of the body they may land upon, as the torso moves from side to side. You may want to add the breath here, coming into the **helicopter breath** by inhaling through the nose at center and exhaling with a deep belly breath "HAA" sound on each side. When you are ready to release, release the breath, then release the movement slowly, finding your way back to center. Pause and notice how the upper body feels. ♟

The upper body exercises can be used before and after practicing your instrument as a way to stretch your muscles out or as a way to rejuvenate. Practicing them in the morning can be a great way to greet the day. Practicing them before you go to bed can be a great way to release and stretch the muscles out so you get a good night sleep. You can use them in the green room before a performance or to periodically stretch during a rehearsal break. You can practice one or two of the exercises anytime throughout the day as a quick fix for releasing tension.

Upper Body Exercises

Exercise	Benefits	Page
Fingers	important to keep limber for performance	55
Lion Pose	stretches and relaxes face muscles	56
Hands	helps prevent overuse injuries	56
Wrist and Arm Rotations	essential for flexibility	57
Shoulders: Tension and Release	exaggerates the tension, then lets it go to feel relaxed	57
Shoulder Circles	releases tension in the shoulders and upper back	57
Neck Circles	releases tension in the neck	58
Shoulder Stretch	opens the space between the shoulder blades	59
Tricep Stretch	stretches the under part of the arm	59
Cow Face Arms	stretches the triceps, shoulders, and chest	60
Eagle Arms	stretches the shoulders and upper back	60
Standing Yoga Mudra	opens the chest and shoulders; stretches the legs	61
Helicopter	energizes and releases tension in the body	63

CHAPTER 6

Spine Exercises

"As a cello player, I have had chronic back problems since high school. Since I started taking yoga, I have been stretching so much more in general, not just when I play, but from when I wake up. My back pain is a lot less frequent, and when it does hurt, I can usually make it go away with the stretches I have learned."

The yogis say, "You are as young as your spine is flexible." It is very important to keep a flexible spine. This is very important for musicians. Think about how much time we spend sitting in rehearsals and classes. We need to keep our flexibility to enjoy a long career of playing our instruments.

In the following exercises, we will be working on the torso area. Many musicians play their instrument in a seated position and develop lower back pain. If you are practicing any instrument in the same position for an extended period of time, it is important to stand up, move around, and release tension. A simple way to release tension in the lower back is to come into a forward bend, either in a standing or seated position. I like the standing position, as you can really allow gravity to release the tension for you by hanging forward with slightly bent knees. If you have any lower back issues, your abdomen could probably use some strengthening as well, so I have also included an exercise for the abdomen at the end of this chapter.

TABLE POSE

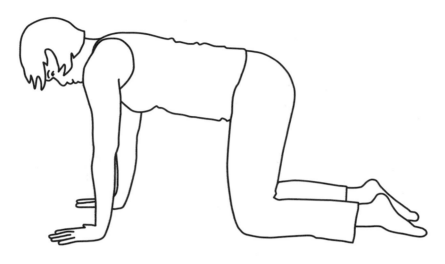

Table pose is a starting position for many exercises and warm-ups for the spine.

🧘 To come into **table pose,** come to your hands and knees. Bring the knees hip-width apart, directly under your hips, and bring the hands shoulder-width apart, spreading the fingers nice and wide, placing them directly under the shoulders. Allow the back and neck to be straight. Feel the elongation from your tailbone to the crown of your head. If you have any wrist sensitivities, you can modify the pose by making fists with the hands, resting on the fists with the backs of the hands facing away from each other. If you need to stay off the wrists entirely, try the **table variation on forearms**, with the elbows directly under the shoulders and the arms reaching straight out in front of you. Find a position that is comfortable for you.

Table Variation on Forearms

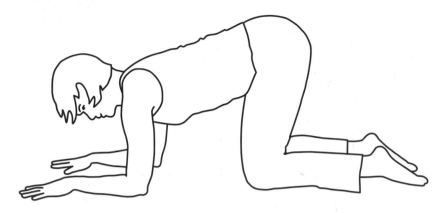

For this **table pose** variation, make sure that the elbows are directly below the shoulders and that the arms are parallel to each other. Spread the fingers wide, placing the entire palm on the ground. Keep the shoulders drawn back and down so that the back does not round in **table pose**.

CAT POSE

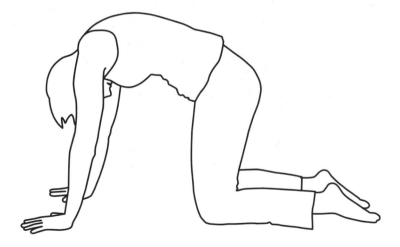

Cat pose stretches the back. From **table pose**, inhale, and as you exhale, press the back of the body up towards the ceiling, dropping the tailbone and crown of the head towards the floor. Squeeze the muscles of the abdomen in and up towards your spine to expel all of the air. You can pause here for several breaths or move directly into **dog pose** on the next inhale.

DOG POSE

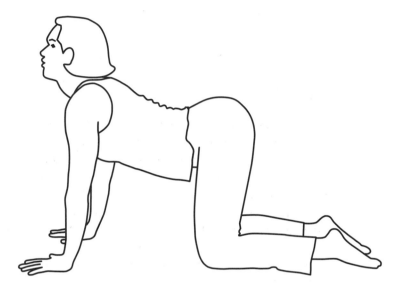

Dog pose stretches the front of the body. From **table pose**, inhale into the **dog pose** by allowing the belly to release towards the floor as the tailbone and crown of the head reach towards the ceiling. The shoulders release down and back, opening the chest area. Pause here for several breaths, or exhale back into the **cat pose**.

CAT AND DOG STRETCH

Inhale in **table pose.** As you exhale, come into the **cat pose**, rounding the back. Inhale as you come into the **dog pose**, allowing the belly to move towards the floor. Continue inhaling and exhaling into these postures for several breaths as you warm up the spine. Feel the breath move the body as you allow the breath to be coordinated with the movement. Feel it as a wave-like motion from the tailbone to the crown of the head. Exhaling into the **cat pose** and inhaling into the **dog pose**, feel all of the movement being generated from the tailbone as each vertebra follows. Allow the breath to be full and deep.

BACK STRENGTHENER

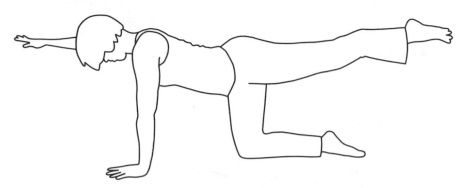

From **table pose**, inhale as you reach your right arm in front of you and extend your left leg behind you, both parallel to the ground. Draw the shoulder blade back and down so that you don't hyperextend the arm. Spread the fingers and toes wide, as you reach through this diagonal stretch, taking several breaths in this position. Exhale the arm and leg back to **table pose**, and pause before switching sides. Inhale the left arm in front of you and the right leg behind you. Take several breaths here, breathing through the diagonal stretch. Keep elongating the spine, reaching through the crown of the head, gazing at the floor. Repeat the entire sequence one or two more times.

OPENING THE SIDES OF THE BODY

From **table pose**, inhale at center. As you exhale, turn to look over your left shoulder, drawing your left hip towards your left shoulder and opening the right side of the body. Pause here for several breaths, breathing into the right rib cage, expanding the rib cage and stretching the right side of the body with the breath. Take one more deep breath into this side, and as you exhale, come back to center. Inhale at center, and exhale as you repeat on the other side.

Opening Sides Variation

Another variation to open the sides of the body more is to take a breath in at center, and as you exhale, walk the hands to the left side, back towards your feet. This will deepen the opening of the right side of the body. Take several deep breaths into this opening. When you are ready to release, inhale and then exhale as you walk the hands back to center. Repeat the same sequence on the other side.

THREAD THE NEEDLE

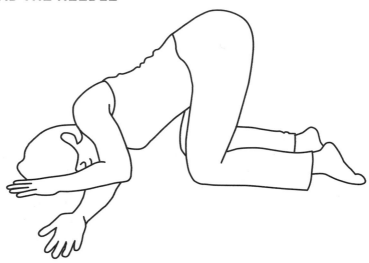

Thread the needle pose opens up the upper back, neck, arms, and shoulders, similar to **eagle arms**. From **table pose**, inhale the right arm straight out to the side. Exhale as you draw the arm under the left, palm facing up. Slide the back of the hand along the ground as far as you can reach, as the arm, shoulder, and side of the head rest on the ground. Keep the chin tucked in towards the chest so that you don't strain the neck. Pause here for several relaxing breaths. Visualize the breath opening and relaxing the space between the shoulder blades. When you are ready to come out, press the left hand into the ground, directly below the left shoulder, and slowly press yourself back to **table pose**. Take a relaxing breath in between, and repeat this sequence on the other side.

Thread the Needle: Hand Variations

In **thread the needle**, the left hand is passive. For these variations, the left hand is in different positions, creating a deeper stretch.

For the first variation, reach the left hand up overhead, sliding the palm along the ground. Breathe into the left armpit, as you relax the left shoulder closer into the ground. This deepens the stretch between the shoulder blades.

For the second variation, inhale the left arm straight up in the air, with your palm facing away from you. This will give a little more weight into the right shoulder, also deepening the stretch.

For the third variation, bend the left elbow, and reach behind your back to grab the top of the right thigh.

FORWARD BEND

Forward bend is excellent for the entire back of the body. You can come into forward bend a number of ways from **mountain pose**. One way to come into the pose is by inhaling the arms straight out to the side and then up overhead with the palms touching, also known as a **sun breath**. As you exhale, keep a slight bend in the knees, bend forward with a flat back, arms extending out to the side and then releasing all the way towards the ground into a **forward bend**.

Allow the head to fully relax. You can gently sway the head back and forth, nodding "yes" and "no." Now is the chance to totally let the head go and relax the muscles of the neck. You can also gently sway the torso from side to side releasing the muscles of the lower back. Relax here for several breaths. If the arms touch the ground, you can clasp the elbows, creating a deeper stretch in the back of the body.

To come back to standing, bend the knees a little deeper as you press through the soles of the feet, and inhale the arms out to the side and overhead with a big **sun breath** and a flat back. When you reach standing with the palms touching overhead, release the arms straight down by your side, back into **mountain pose**. Whenever you come out of **forward bend**, concentrate on pushing into the ground with the soles of the feet, to take strain and pressure off the lower back. Also, keeping a slight bend in the knees will help protect the lower back.

If it is comfortable for the back, another variation for coming into **forward bend** from **mountain pose** is to keep a slight bend in the knees as you slowly roll down one vertebra at a time. Start by drawing your chin towards your chest, continuing to roll all the way down the spine. Hang in **forward bend** for several breaths. To come out of the pose, bend the knees a little deeper, and slowly begin to roll back into a standing position, as you press into the soles of the feet, stacking one vertebra at a time. Once you reach standing position, pause and notice how you feel. ♟

EXTENDED CHILD POSE

Extended child pose helps to rejuvenate the entire body. It is especially helpful to release tension in the back and spine. It is very calming and relaxing. It is a nice posture to practice before retiring to bed or any time your lower back needs release.

♟ Start this posture by coming into **table pose** on your hands and knees. Your hands are directly under your shoulders, and your knees are directly under your hips. Lengthen the spine through the crown of your head and tailbone. Take in a deep breath. As you exhale, lower your buttocks to your heels. Allow your belly to rest on or between the thighs. Keep your arms extended overhead, fingers spread wide, as you rest your forehead on the ground. Even though the arms are stretched overhead, always keep the shoulder blades drawing down and towards each other, so that you don't hyperextend the shoulders. Take long, slow breaths, consciously relaxing deeper into the pose on the exhales. Imagine you could breathe into the armpits, deepening the stretch in the torso and arms. Either stay in this position or come into the relaxed **child pose** by bringing your arms back down by your side, hands by the feet, and palms facing up toward the ceiling. Allow the upper back and shoulders to fully release as the back rounds. Relax here for as long as you would like. When you are ready to come out of this posture, bring your hands directly under your shoulders, and slowly press yourself back into **table pose**.

Extended Child Pose Variation

If **extended child pose** is not comfortable for you, you can also do a variation by making fists with your hands, stacking the fists on each other, and resting your head on your fists. If your buttocks do not touch your heels, you can put a pillow or a cushion under your buttocks and rest on that. ♟

SPINAL TWIST

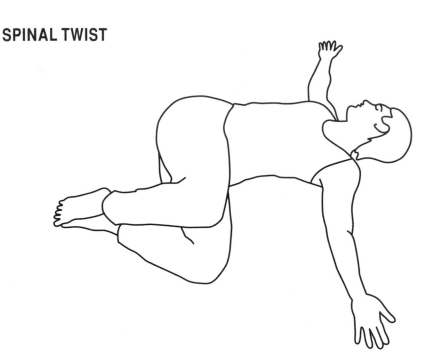

Spinal twists are good for aligning the spine and are a great way to release toxins in the body. There are many variations of spinal twist. Here we will learn a basic reclining spinal twist. When we get to the Kundalini wake-up routine, we will learn another variation of a spinal twist. I like to end my routines with a spinal twist before I come into the final relaxation pose, shavasana (see chapter 9).

♟ Begin by lying on your back. Draw both knees into your chest, curling yourself in a ball. Take a few breaths, releasing the lower back. Keep the knees in towards the chest as you extend your arms out to the sides of the body in a T position at shoulder height or slightly lower. Face the palms up to allow the chest to stay open.

Inhale, and as you exhale, slowly bring your knees down to the left side. Try to keep your right shoulder relaxing into the ground. Make any adjustments to allow this shoulder to release into the ground. You might need to draw the knees off the ground a bit more or move the knees away from the elbows a little more. Turn to look over your right fingertips to bring the twist into the entire spine. If that is uncomfortable for the neck, keep looking straight up towards the ceiling. Breathe deeply, and as you exhale, relax into the stretch. Stay here for several breaths, relaxing fully into the stretch, allowing gravity to work for you.

When you feel that this side has been stretched enough, turn to look back to the ceiling, take a breath in. On an exhale, engage your core, and bring the knees up to center in preparation for the other side. Take a breath in at center. As you exhale, slowly release the legs to the other side, and repeat the same sequence. 🧘

STAFF POSE

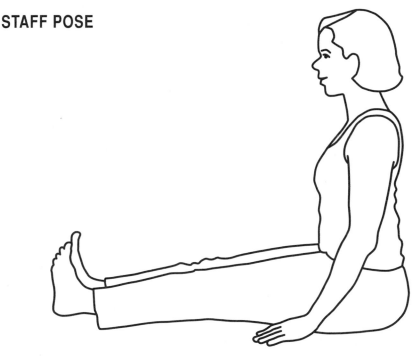

Staff pose is similar to **mountain pose** in that you are looking for a tall, straight spine with your shoulders relaxed. It is difficult for many people to come into the full staff pose, right away, particularly if their hamstrings are very tight. If you practice it with variations, you will be able to stretch the hamstrings and strengthen the muscles of the back and maybe eventually come into the full pose.

You will get the full benefit of any pose if you start it at a point where you can have proper alignment and find a challenging stretch in which you can still breathe deeply and fully. For staff pose, first, it is important to keep the back straight. Over time, you can work on straightening the legs.

🧘 To begin **staff pose**, try sitting on the floor with your pelvis tilted slightly forward to get the back straight. The legs should be straight and the spine tall. Flex your feet, so that the toes point towards the ceiling. The heels should press away from you. It is helpful to see yourself in the mirror or have another person check to see if you have a straight spine. You can also use the support of the wall to feel if the spine is straight. Keep the buttocks, shoulder blades, and back of the head touching the wall, then come a few inches away from the wall and see if you can keep the same feeling of the supported spine. Many times, we think we are doing certain poses properly, but when we check ourselves, we find that we are not where we thought we were. If you find that this position is too painful or that your spine is rounded, you will need to work with some of the variations listed below.

Hold **staff pose** for several breaths, and notice which muscles are working to keep you in this position. If this position is not difficult for you, you can intensify the pose by coming into a **forward bend**. Make sure you bend from the waist, keep the back straight without rounding the spine, and lead with your chest. Inhale as you back away from the stretch, and exhale as you come deeper into the stretch, working with your edge. Work in this way for about 30 seconds to 1 minute. When you are ready to release from the pose, inhale back up, and exhale by bending forward and rounding the spine, and then release the head down. This will relax and stretch out the entire back of the body. Relax here for several breaths.

Staff Pose Variations

Keeping a slight bend in the knees will help you tilt the pelvis forward, to keep the back in alignment. If you are using a yoga mat, you can also roll it up and sit on the edge to tilt the pelvis forward to get a straight back. Or, sit up against a wall with your buttocks touching the wall, back straight, and legs straight. If your hamstrings are very tight, you will need to keep a slight bend in the knees.

STAFF POSE WITH ARMS EXTENDED

Another way to intensify **staff pose** is to extend the arms straight overhead. Inhale the arms overhead with the fingers spread wide, the palms facing towards each other. Keep the inner elbows close by the ears, relaxing the shoulder blades down and back. Work with the breath, inhaling as you back away from the stretch and exhaling as you bend forward, to deepen the stretch. Keep the back straight. If it gets too intense, release the arms back down by your side. Hold this position for several breaths. To release, round the spine and relax in a **forward bend** for a few more breaths. ♟

WATER WHEELS

If your back bothers you, your abdomen probably needs some work as well. It is important to strengthen both the back and front of the body. The **water wheels** exercise is a good way to strengthen the muscles of the abdomen.

♟ Begin this exercise lying on your back. Lift your legs off the ground and press the soles of your feet toward the ceiling. This should look like the **staff pose**, except that you are lying on your back with your legs up in the air. Bring your hands under the buttocks slightly to help support your lower back. Keep the lower back pressing into the floor during the whole exercise. Engage the muscles of the abdomen. Take a breath in, and as you exhale, slowly lower your legs towards the ground, keeping the legs as straight as possible. If this is too difficult at first, you can keep a slight bend in the knees, gradually working towards straightening the legs over time. Keep the lower back pressing into the ground the entire time, and just before it starts to round and lift off the ground, bend the knees, bringing them in towards the chest, then bring them up in the air for another round.

The slower you release your legs towards the ground, the more you will be working the muscles of the abdomen. You can also take several breaths to release the legs towards the ground. Keep breathing the entire exercise. Do not hold the breath. Do several rounds of this, then to release from the exercise, bring the knees into the chest and wrap your arms around your legs, squeezing them in to release the lower back. This exercise will help strengthen the abdominal muscles, helping to release low back pain. ♟

Spine Exercises

Exercise	Benefits	Page
Table Pose	elongates the spine	69
Cat and Dog Stretch	opens front and back of the body	71
Back Strengthener	strengthens the entire back	72
Opening the Sides of the Body	expands rib cage for breath	72
Thread the Needle	stretches the shoulders, upper back, arms, and neck	73
Forward Bend	lengthens the entire back of the body	74
Extended Child Pose	stretches the spine and relaxes the nervous system	75
Spinal Twist	spinal alignment	76
Staff Pose	strengthens hamstrings and back; improves posture	77
Staff Pose with Arms Extended	strengthens the entire back of the body	79
Water Wheels	strengthens abdominal muscles	80

CHAPTER 7

Lower Body Exercises

Warrior postures can be very grounding if you focus on rooting through the bottoms of the feet, feeling the connection with the earth beneath you. If we are too much in our heads, we lose our connection with our feet and we feel that we are not centered. Have you ever had that feeling when you are on stage of being a little overwhelmed, or the mind chatter is trying to take you away on a story, or your legs feel shaky? Practicing the lower body exercises will help give you strength and flexibility in your legs and will help you feel more grounded and centered.

Practicing these exercises will also strengthen the mind-body connection. Even if you play your instrument in a seated position, the same principles will apply with rooting and grounding, feeling solid, strong, and secure through your feet and sitting bones.

There are many ways to come into the various standing postures. We will start all of these in **mountain pose**, stepping one leg out at a time.

WARRIOR 1

🧘 Come into **mountain pose**, bring your hands to your hips, and take a deep breath in. As you exhale, step your left foot straight back into a lunge. Keep your left heel pressing back towards the ground to elongate and straighten the leg. Keep your right knee bent making sure that the knee is directly aligned above your ankle to protect the knee. Hips face forward. Keep your arms by your side if you have shoulder sensitivity. Otherwise, you can inhale your arms up overhead, shoulder width apart, palms facing towards each other drawing your shoulders back and down. Spread the fingers nice and wide, and imagine you are gathering energy from above you, filling the whole body as you ground through your feet in the posture. Turn the corners of your mouth up slightly, and notice how that can uplift your mood. Take three to five deep breaths in this position. To release from the posture, bring your arms back down to your hips and take a deep breath in. As you exhale, shift your weight to your right foot and step the left foot forward into **mountain pose**. Pause for a moment, and notice the difference between your right and left side; then do the same sequence the other side.

Another variation for releasing the posture is to take a deep breath in, and as you exhale, swing your arms down and back, palms facing towards the ground, bending forward to allow your chest to rest on your thigh. Take a breath in as you swing your arms forward and step your left foot forward, coming back into **mountain pose**. Pause for a moment, and then do the same sequence the other side.

A variation you may want to try while you are in the **warrior posture** is to clasp your hands behind your head, drawing your elbows back. This helps to open the chest and also makes it easier on the shoulders.

WARRIOR 2

From **mountain pose**, take a wide step to the right, keeping your feet parallel. Turn your right foot out to form a 90° angle with your left foot. Now, turn your left foot in to about a 45° angle. Bend your right knee so that it is placed directly above the ankle. Inhale the arms straight out to the sides at shoulder height. Keep your shoulders relaxed as you turn your palms to face up towards the ceiling. Notice how that opens the chest and draws the shoulder blades down and back. Keep this opening in the chest as you turn your palms to face the floor. Elongate through the fingertips as you ground through your feet and lengthen through the crown of your head. Turn to look at your right fingertips. The *drishdi*, or point of focus, should be at your right middle finger. Hold for several breaths.

It is important to remember to keep the right knee directly over the ankle. Many people let this knee cave in to the left, which puts pressure on the knee. Keep the knee pressing back to the right. This will open the hips more and also protect the knee. You can move into **side angle warrior posture** or release from the posture from this position.

To release from the posture, straighten the right leg and exhale the arms down by your sides. Turn the feet back to being parallel, and step back into **mountain pose**. Repeat the same sequence on the other side.

SIDE ANGLE WARRIOR

From **warrior 2**, inhale, and as you exhale, bend your right elbow and place the right forearm gently on your right thigh. Reach your left arm up overhead, reaching towards the right side. The left palm should be facing towards the ground. Relax the left shoulder back and down as you open the chest slightly towards the ceiling. Feel a long line of energy from the outside of the left foot to the left fingertips. The *drishdi* can be looking down at your foot, straight out to the wall, or up to the ceiling. Ground through the feet, keep the right knee pressing back, and make sure it is directly above the ankle. You can move into **reversed warrior posture** or release from the posture and repeat the sequence on the other side.

REVERSED WARRIOR

From **side angle warrior**, inhale back to **warrior 2**, and let the left arm slide down the left leg as the right arm reaches up toward the ceiling. Look up to your right palm, which faces behind you. Take several breaths and when you are ready to release, exhale the arms back to **warrior 2**, and repeat the same sequence on the other side. ♟

TRIANGLE

The triangle posture can help with flexibility in the torso and hips and also helps to elongate the spine.

🧘 From **warrior** 2 position, straighten your right leg, keeping a slight bend in the knee. Never lock your joints, always keep a slight bend to protect the joints. Maintain a slight tuck to the tailbone and engage your core as you exhale, reaching your right arm straight out in front of you. You can imagine that you are sliding this arm across a tabletop, reaching as far as you can as you bend from the waist. From here, simply rotate the arms so that the right arm reaches towards the floor and the left arm reaches towards the ceiling, palms face towards the wall in front of you. Do not try to reach the floor or let your right arm rest on your shin or ankle. Keep elongating out of the waist, opening the left side of the chest slightly towards the ceiling.

There are some helpful things you can do to help get the proper posture. One is to imagine that your body was placed in between two planes of glass. The common tendency in this posture is to bend forward, allowing the buttocks to hit the plane of glass behind you and your head to hit the plane of glass in front of you. You can also try practicing this with the support of the wall behind you to get the feeling of reaching up and out of the waist. ♟

PUT IT INTO PRACTICE

Here is an exercise routine that is good to practice to develop a sense of grounding through the lower body. I have listed all of the warrior postures in sequence. You can do each one individually or move from one pose right into the next pose as this routine shows.

♟ Start in **mountain pose** with the feet hip-width apart, knees slightly bent, tailbone slightly tucked. Relax the shoulder blades back and down as the chest lifts and opens. Elongate from the crown of your head. Connect with your **full yogic breath**.

When you are ready, bring your hands to your hips. On an exhale, step your left leg straight back into **warrior 1**. Keep the hips facing forward. Press through the back heel. Keep your arms on the hips or inhale the arms up overhead into the full **warrior 1** pose. Keep the shoulders drawing back and down, palms facing each other. Energize the posture by reaching through the fingertips, and spreading the fingers wide apart. Stay here for several breaths as you strengthen the muscles of the legs.

On the next exhale, place the back foot on the ground with the toes pointing towards the front at about a 45-degree angle. Hips still face to the front. This is a variation for the feet for **warrior 1**.

Inhale, then exhale into **warrior 2**, hips open up to the left side. Make sure that your right knee is aligned directly above the right ankle. Don't let the knee drift to the left side. Press it to the right side slightly. Right arm reaches in front as the left arm reaches back. Arms are parallel to the ground. Relax the shoulders as you draw the shoulder blades back and down. Imagine you are gathering all the energy you need for your performance through your fingertips. To make sure the chest is open, rotate the palms to face up towards the ceiling. Keep this opening in the chest as you rotate the palms back down. Your *drishdi* should be at the right middle fingertip. Pause here for several breaths.

From **warrior 2**, bend your right elbow, and place your right forearm lightly on the right thigh coming into **side angle warrior**. Left arm reaches up and overhead. Feel the long line of energy through the entire left side of the body. Pause here for a breath or two.

Inhale into **reversed warrior**. Left arm slides down the left leg as the right arm reaches up towards the ceiling. Gaze up to the ceiling as you pause here for a few breaths. Inhale back to **warrior 2** for one breath, then into **warrior 1** for one breath. Bring the arms back to your hips and inhale as you step the back leg to meet the front standing in **mountain pose**. Pause here for several breaths to notice the difference between the two sides. Repeat the entire sequence on the right side. 🧘

Lower Body Exercises

Exercise	Benefits	Page
Warrior 1	helps to stand your ground; strengthens legs, hips, and shoulders	83
Warrior 2	helps to open hips, chest, and shoulders	84
Side Angle Warrior	opens hips, shoulders, and the entire side of the body	85
Reversed Warrior	opens up rib cage, strengthens lower body	86
Triangle	strengthens core of the body, legs, hips, and shoulders	87

CHAPTER 8

Exercises for Balance, Focus, and Concentration

"By performing yoga, I felt that my concentration in everyday life, such as practicing, working out, or studying, was improved. Concentration, that's what I felt from yoga. Yoga helped me with mental concentration and relaxation with my body, especially with the many unique positions and breathing exercises."

Balancing exercises help increase focus and concentration. They also help our mind-body connection. Balancing postures can be challenging, and whenever we find something challenging, the volume of the mind chatter starts to increase and the breath becomes shallow. As you practice the exercises, you will begin to notice that they are easier some days than others. This is natural, and it varies depending on how you are feeling or how you are thinking. It is important to keep the judges away and be in the present moment—be with the experience.

There are many stages to these postures, and it is important that you don't move into the next stage until you can become fully focused on the focal point (*drishdi*) and keep the breath deep and steady. If you fall out of a pose, just come back and give it another try. It is also fun to experiment by swaying gently with the breeze to see how far you can go before you fall out of position. When you fall, see how gracefully you can fall. I will tell my students that if it is a windy day, allow the winds to be there, don't fight it. Go with it and breathe. Some days, you might feel like you are in a hurricane. If you start to feel tension, exhale it away with a sigh. Notice what the mind is saying as you are in the pose, breathe into it, and let it go on the exhale. Don't become engaged in the mind chatter.

I think that balancing poses are the most important poses to practice regularly because they immediately bring you in touch with the mind-body connection. These poses are similar to being on stage. You can see right away what the mind chatter is all about when you come into the pose or when you go on stage. Let it all be there, don't push it away, but stay fully present grounding to the earth, elongating through the spine and staying connected to your deep breath.

BALANCING POSE WARM-UP

Start the following exercises in **mountain pose**. It is helpful to find a focal point (*drishdi*) in front of you at eye level, to focus the eyes and help with concentration. Connect with your **full yogic breath**. Bring all of your weight into your left leg, growing the roots deep beneath the earth. Keep a slight bend in the left knee. Allow your right leg to lift off the ground a bit, and begin to rotate the ankle a few times in one direction, then in the opposite direction. Lift the leg a little higher, and rotate from the knee in one direction, then in the opposite direction. Rotate from the hip in one direction and in the other direction. Release this leg, and exhale with a sigh. Pause for a moment to notice the difference between the two sides, then repeat the same sequence on the other side. Keep the breath flowing throughout the entire exercise.

TREE

Shift all of your weight into your left leg, grounding through the entire foot, growing your roots deep beneath the earth. Keep a slight bend in the left knee. Start the **tree** posture by gently placing the right heel on the left side of the ankle with the toes touching the ground. Bring your hands into **prayer position** in front of the chest, palms touching, and thumbs pressing gently against your heart center. Find a steady, deep breath in this position before you come into the full **tree** posture. If you are feeling at all unsteady, this may be all that you do for this day. Don't move into the full posture if you are not feeling steady. It's better to be in this first position and stay connected to your breath, keeping a steady focus.

To come into the full **tree** posture, place the bottom of the right foot on the calf or inner thigh of your left leg. Do not place it on the knee, as knees are vulnerable joints. Keep the right knee pointing out to the side as much as possible, opening up the hip and groin area. Place the hands in prayer position. If you can stay in this position with a steady breath, you can try experimenting with different hand variations.

Inhale the arms over your head, growing your branches. Keep the shoulders releasing back and down. Hands can be in **prayer position** up overhead, or **temple position** by clasping the hands together with the pointer fingers reaching up to the sky, or spread the arms wide apart with palms facing each other and fingers spread wide apart. No matter what position you are in, make sure you are breathing deeply and that your shoulders are relaxed.

The common tendency with balancing postures is to hold the breath. Keep the breath flowing. Stay in this position for several breaths, experimenting with different arm or leg variations. There are many different types of trees in the forest, so you can be your own unique tree. When you are ready to release the posture, come out slowly, with as much control as possible. Allow your hands to come back to **prayer position**. Release the leg down. Pause, exhale that side away with a big sigh, then repeat the same sequence on the other side.

WARRIOR 3

From **mountain pose**, keep your arms down by your sides with the palms facing forward, fingers spread wide. Bring all of your weight into your right leg, keeping a slight bend in the knee, growing the roots deep beneath the earth. Bring the left foot behind about a foot and lightly touch the toes to the ground. On an exhale, let the left leg lift off the ground behind you, allowing the torso to move slowly towards being parallel with the ground. It is not important to become perfectly parallel with the ground, but to keep one long line from the toe of the left foot to the tip of the head. When you are ready to release, keep the torso in one long line, and slowly come back to standing position. Take a few breaths to ground yourself, then reverse sides.

Warrior 3 Arm Variation

From **warrior 3** pose, extend your arms so that they are reaching overhead, drawing the shoulders back and down as you reach. Imagine the whole front of the body being lifted and supported. Lengthen through the back leg by pointing through the toes or flexing the foot and reaching through the heel. Elongate through the crown of the head, and spread the fingers wide, palms facing each other.

Another way to enter the posture is from **mountain pose**. Shift your weight on the balancing leg, and curl your toes under on the leg you are going to lift. Putting a little weight into the top of the foot can give a nice stretch to the top of the foot and ankle before you come into the posture. Reach the arms overhead, shoulders releasing down and back. Palms face each other with fingers spread wide apart, or bring your hands into **temple position**. Feel the elongation, and lift through the front of the body as you move into

warrior 3. Lift the leg behind you as you reach the arms in front of you, moving towards a parallel position to the floor. Pause here for several breaths, then release back into **mountain pose**.

EAGLE POSE

From **mountain pose**, come into **eagle arms**, as described in chapter 5 (p. 60), crossing the right arm under the left. Bend the knees deeply as if you were sitting on a chair. Keep a slight tuck to the tailbone to protect the lower back. The deeper the bend, the easier it is to get the legs into position. Cross the right leg over the left. You may need to rest the toes on the ground if you need more stability. If you can, keep the toes off the ground. If you feel stable here, then try tucking the toes behind the calf. This is the full **eagle pose**.

Try to align the elbows directly above the knees. Squeeze the arms together, and squeeze the legs together. Hold here for several breaths, and when you are ready, slowly release legs and arms, coming back into a standing position. Shake or wiggle out any tension, take in a deep breath, and sigh it out. Pause and notice the difference between the two sides. Repeat the entire sequence on the other side. ♟

If we can stay calm, centered, and focused when we practice our balancing postures on our yoga mat, we will be able to stay focused when we have to perform. We will understand and know when the mind chatter comes, and we can let it go and be fully present with our task at hand.

Balance, Focus, and Concentration Exercises

Exercise	Benefits	Page
Balancing Pose	warm-up, prepares mind and body for balancing exercises	92
Tree	opens hips; strengthens legs; lengthens spine	93
Warrior 3	lengthens entire body; strengthens legs, shoulders, and back	94
Eagle Pose	stretches hips, upper back, and shoulders; strengthens legs	96

CHAPTER 9

Taking Care of Yourself

The life of a musician can be a very stressful one. Many are dealing with how to make enough money as a musician, where the next gig is coming from, or how to get more students. Others may be dealing with how to stay at their top level of performance with so many gigs and a heavy traveling schedule, or how to stay fresh for each performance, playing the same show night after night. Maybe you are looking for ways to help relieve your nerves for an audition or a performance. Whatever you are searching for to improve your life as a musician, the tools that you will learn in this book can help ease your way.

In addition to the specific exercises and areas of the body you can work on, I would also like to share with you specific routines that I find very helpful in my daily life. Feel free to modify or take parts of these routines to see what works best for you.

KUNDALINI WAKE-UP ROUTINE

I have adapted the following wake-up routine from the Kundalini yoga tradition. Kundalini yoga exercises are relatively repetitive, often repeating one particular move over and over again. The following exercises are designed to get you going in the morning. Practice them before you get out of bed to wake up the entire body nice and gradually, then see how different you feel during your day. Do each exercise for about 30 seconds to 1 minute, or until you feel you have done enough. Start each exercise lying on your back with your arms by your side. It is important to keep each movement going until you start the next movement. If you stop moving, you may start to drift back to sleep.

Once you practice this routine a few times, it is easy to remember. There is a total of seven exercises. There are two for the lower body, two for the upper body, two for the torso, and one for the entire back of the body. If you forget the order, it's no big deal. Just keep moving on to something that you remember. You can learn the exercises by first trying them one at a time, then start to visualize yourself doing them a few times. Then, do them when you wake up the next day, and see how much you remember.

1. **Feet.** Move one foot at a time, pointing the toes towards you and then away from you. You can also wiggle your toes at the same time. Keep this back-and-forth motion going until you feel that the feet, toes, and ankles are starting to wake up.

2. **Legs.** Release the movement of the feet, and start bending one knee at a time as you slide the bottoms of the feet along the bed.

3. **Shoulders.** Release the movement of the legs, and start to slide one shoulder up to your ear while the other slides down towards your toes. Alternate back and forth.

4. **Neck.** Release the movement of the shoulders, and bend your knees towards your chest, curling yourself up into a ball as you wrap your arms around your legs and tuck your chin towards your chest. Begin to rotate your head slowly in circles in one direction, 3 to 5 times, then slowly in the other direction, 3 to 5 times, loosening up the muscles of the neck.

5. **Abdomen/Face.** Release the legs, coming back in the lying down position. Point your toes away from you, and point your fingers towards your toes. Engage the muscles of your abdomen as you begin to lift your upper body and legs off the bed. Use your core, abdominal strength to lift you up. Reach towards your toes, spreading the fingers and toes wide to enliven them. At the same time, engage the muscles of your face by coming into the **lion pose.** Open the mouth wide, stick out the tongue toward your chin, and open the eyes wide, looking straight up to wake up the face. Hold this position until you feel the belly "burn," then release back to your bed, rest for a breath or two, then repeat this exercise two more times.

6. **Spine.** Now we move on to a **spinal twist,** otherwise known as the "cat stretch" in Kundalini yoga. Bring the arms out from the body into a T position. Bend the right knee, and place it on the left thigh. Allow the right knee to come to the left side of the body, giving yourself a nice spinal twist. Do not worry if that knee does not come all the way to touch the bed. Try to keep your right shoulder in contact with the bed. You can turn the head to gaze out over the right fingertips to bring the twist all the way up your spine. Hold this position for about 30 seconds. To release, bring the head back to center, bring the right knee back up and straighten the leg. Now do the twist on the other side.

7. **Entire Back of the Body: Forward Bend.** Come up gradually to a seated position, and allow the upper body to round over the legs into a **forward bend**. Relax the head down, and breathe into the back of the body for several breaths. Come up very slowly, pause for a moment, step out of bed, and now you are ready to start your day. 🧘

After you have practiced each of the exercises, you can practice visualizing yourself doing the exercises in this order. The visual practice will help you remember the exercises as well as the order of the exercises, so that when you wake up, it will become second nature as to what you should do before getting out of bed. Visualize:

1. Feet (lower body)
2. Legs (lower body)
3. Shoulders (upper body)
4. Neck (upper body)
5. Abdomen/Face (torso)
6. Spine (torso)
7. Entire Back of the Body (whole body)

TAPPING AND SELF MASSAGE

These exercises are wonderful to do in the morning to wake up your whole body. They are also nice to do when you are feeling a little sluggish. You can practice the entire routine from head to toe, or if you want to practice parts for different areas of the body, you can do that as well. Try it as a break during your instrumental practice; it can help enliven the body. If you are thinking too hard, it's nice to do the head part.

This routine helps to invigorate the entire body and get the energy moving and flowing. It helps to wake up the meridian or energy channels of the body and get fresh blood flowing.

Come into a seated position, either in a cross-legged position or on a chair. We will start this sequence from the head moving down to the toes.

🧘 Start by rubbing your palms together. Once you have generated enough heat in the palms, gently place your palms over your eyes. Feel the heat from the palms penetrating your eyes, relaxing all the muscles of the eyes and face. Keep your shoulders nice and relaxed as you gently rest the hands over the eyes for a few long, slow breaths. Once you feel relaxation with the whole body, start to massage the forehead making little circles with your fingertips, relaxing the muscles of your forehead. Start to move to the eyebrows and temples, then the cheeks and nose. Lightly tap from the cheeks to your nose, awakening the sinuses. This tapping can also help loosen the sinuses if you feel you have a cold coming on.

Loosen the jaw by opening the mouth and relaxing the tongue. Feel the indentation between the jawbones. Make circles with the fingertips, loosening up the muscles here. This area can be tight and sore for many people. This exercise is also good to practice before you go to bed if you tend to clench your teeth at night. Gently tug along the jawbone towards the chin. Continuing on with the face massage, move to the ears. Gently tug on the outer edges of the ears, from the lobes to the tops of the ears and back a few times waking up the ears.

Massage the whole head with your fingertips, loosening up the energy here. Imagine you were in the shower, washing your hair. Don't worry about messing up your hair. You can fix it later.

I like to do this exercise as a little break if there is too much on my mind or I have been studying or thinking too much. It helps to move the energy and refresh me.

Continue the massage moving down to the neck and shoulders. Massage the muscles along the neck, then along the tops of the shoulders. Massage, tap, or knead these areas, doing whatever feels good.

Moving on to what I call the Tarzan and Jane move. Make loose fists and gently tap your chest, just below the collarbones. Take a deep breath in and let it out with a big sound. Do this at least another time or two. It's great to produce sounds to get the energy flowing and also to release stagnation and tension in the body.

Continue the following exercises with loose fists, or use the palms of the hands if that is more comfortable.

Gently tap down and up each arm, moving toward the fingertips and back up toward the shoulder. Make sure to tap the top, bottom, and sides of the arm. Move on to the other arm, waking up both arms.

Continue this light tapping on the back of the body from just below the shoulder blades down to the buttocks. Lightly tap along the kidney area, releasing any stagnation here.

Then, relax the muscles of the abdomen. Make a circular motion with your palm to rub the belly. As you look at your belly, make the circles in a clockwise motion, as this is the way the energy flows for digestion and elimination. (Start at the top, move to the left, down and to the right, going around and around.) We tend to hold these muscles tight throughout the day, as this is where we hold much of our armor. It is important to relax here, softening the muscles of the belly.

If you are sitting on the ground in a cross-legged position, release the legs out in front of you and shake them out. Begin the tapping motion up and down each leg from the top of the leg down to the toes, making sure to get the top, bottom, and sides of the legs and the top and bottom of the feet.

If you have a little extra time, massage the bottoms of each foot with your thumbs, running the thumb along your arches. Give each toe a little tug, and you are ready to complete the series.

Now, shake the whole body out while taking in a deep breath, then exhale, making lots of sounds. Take in a few deep breaths, and let everything go with lots of sound. Let go of tension, negative thoughts—anything that is no longer serving you, just let it all go. Shake it and sound it away. Then, notice how you feel. Enjoy! ♣

EYE EXERCISES

The eyes tend to be neglected or taken for granted. They can also become fatigued, and should also be exercised. If you spend a lot of time at your computer or reading music or books, it is important to take breaks for the eyes during these activities to reduce eyestrain and strengthen the eye muscles. The following exercises are helpful.

Eyestrain Reducer

♟ The first exercise is very simple. Whenever you are at your computer or reading music or a book, take a few moments to look far away periodically. Let your eyes focus on the furthest possible point that you can see. This will allow your eyes to relax. If you are working at the computer and need a reminder to take a break, you can set an alarm. Whenever you hear it, look away for a few moments, allowing your eyes to adjust to a point at a further distance away. This can greatly reduce eyestrain. ♟

Eye Strengthener: Clock Exercise

In this exercise, we will be visualizing the numbers of the clock, moving our eyes around it in both directions, to help strengthen the eye muscles as well as release eye fatigue.

♟ Sit in a comfortable position with your spine tall, grounding through the sitting bones, lengthening through the crown of the head, shoulders relaxed, face and jaw soft.

Rub your palms together to generate heat. Once you have enough heat in the palms, allow your palms to rest gently over your eyes, cupping the eyes with your hands. Connect with your breath, and breathe long, slow breaths, making sure you are staying relaxed. Pay special attention to relaxing the muscles of your eyes, face, neck, and shoulders. Once you feel the relaxation, remove your hands from your eyes placing them in your lap.

Open your eyes, and look far away at a point straight in front of you. Inhale and exhale. Now, look straight up. This is 12:00. Start going around the clock in a clockwise direction, moving slowly to each number, saying to yourself, 1:00, 2:00, 3:00 (now you should be looking straight out to the right), 4:00, 5:00, 6:00 (now you should be looking straight down towards the ground), 7:00, 8:00, 9:00 (now you are looking straight out to the left), 10:00, 11:00, and back to 12:00 (looking straight up). Look straight in front of you and then close your eyes to relax your eye muscles. Take in a deep breath, and sigh it out, pausing here for a few breaths with your eyes closed.

Open your eyes, looking straight ahead. Now we will reverse the direction of our eye circles, moving counterclockwise. Look up to 12:00 then 11:00, 10:00, 9:00, etc. all the way around the clock. Once you reach 12:00, look straight ahead, close your eyes, take in a deep breath, and exhale it away with a sigh. Do this same sequence going in a clockwise then counterclockwise direction, pausing in between with a few long, slow, deep breaths to relax the eye muscles. ♟

POSTURES FOR RELAXATION AND REJUVENATION

Relaxation is the most important part of a yoga practice routine. When we come into our final relaxation pose after doing our warm-ups and postures, it is important to take the time to relax and let go. This time allows the body to integrate all of the postures that have been practiced. After a long day of rehearsal or practice, it's time to let go. Don't underestimate the power of relaxation. It teaches the body and the mind to release and let go.

RELAXATION (*SHAVASANA*)

There is something very powerful to hearing your own voice telling you to relax. I recommend recording the following paragraphs so that you can practice to the sound of your own voice. When you do this, speak slowly and with a relaxed voice. Pause for a moment or two between each body part.

♟ To prepare the body for relaxation, you might want to find a blanket, as the body will cool down when activity stops. You may also want to use an eyebag to block out any light. Come into a position lying on your back with your feet a little wider than hip-width apart. Bring your arms about a 45-degree angle away from your body, palms facing up in a receptive position. To get the arms to face up, it is important to draw your shoulders back and down, just as in **mountain pose**. This will open the chest and the palms.

Take in a deep breath and exhale with a sigh. You may want to do this a few times to really release any tension that is still there.

Start to feel the whole body release into the support of the floor beneath you. Consciously release the muscles of each part of the body, starting with the feet, and moving to the head. Relax the tops and bottoms of the feet, the toes, and ankles. Release the shins and calves, the muscles around the knees, the thighs and hamstrings. Relax the hips and buttocks, and feel the whole lower body release into the ground. Soften the belly, and release the lower back and mid back. Soften the chest, and release the upper back and shoulders, feeling the torso relax and let go. Allow the arms to become heavy, releasing the upper arms, elbows, lower arms, wrists, tops of the hands, backs of the hands, and fingertips. Relax the face muscles, releasing the jaw and softening the tongue. Soften all of the muscles around the eyes, temples, eyebrows, and forehead. Relax the scalp. Take the next 5 to 10 minutes to totally release, relax, and let go. Allow all the sounds around you to float further and further away.

When you are ready to come out of **shavasana**, bring your attention back to the breath. Begin to deepen the breath, inhaling into the belly. Gently turn the head from side to side. Wiggle your fingers and toes, and rotate your wrists and ankles, arms and legs. Draw the arms up overhead to give a good stretch to the entire body from the fingertips to the toes. Draw the knees into the chest and roll over to one side, lying in a fetal position. Pause here for a moment.

With the least amount of effort as possible, either with the eyes still closed or with a soft gaze, use your arms to lift yourself back into seated position by placing the top hand into the ground, rotating your torso around the legs, and using the other hand for support to lift yourself up gradually into a seated position. Connect the sitting bones with the ground beneath you, elongating through the crown of the head, shoulders relaxed back and down. Pause here for a moment, and notice how you feel. Notice how the body feels. Notice how the mind feels.

You may want to end your practice with three rounds of om, which is how many yoga classes end. Om is a universal sound and is produced in three parts; ahhh, oooo, mmm. Feel the vibration of sound in your whole body.

You may also want to end your practice by drawing your hands in front of heart center in **prayer position**. Draw the chin slightly toward yourself, bowing to your internal self. Give thanks to your body, your body that works so hard for you every day. Also find something else in your life that you are thankful for and offer that as a sense of gratitude and appreciation for what you have. In my classes, we end our practice by saying "Namaste." I see the light within you. ♟

Another form of practicing *shavasana* is to practice tension and release with each body part. Tense each body part, and lift it off the floor slightly. Then release it and let it go, as you totally relax it into the support of the floor. Start from the feet, moving up through the legs, torso, and arms, then finally the muscles of the face. Relax the mind, and rest for 5 to 10 minutes.

RELAXATION FOR A GOOD NIGHT'S SLEEP

♟ Practice this before you go to bed so that you can feel well rested the next morning. It is also helpful for relaxing the body and mind if you have insomnia.

If you have been sitting or standing a lot, practicing inversions will allow the blood to flow in the opposite direction. A supportive inversion is **legs-up-the–wall pose**. To come into this pose, lie on your back with the buttocks close to the wall. Extend your legs up the wall, and rest your heels on the wall. Stay here for several minutes, concentrating on a relaxing, slow breath. When you are ready to release, bend the knees into the chest, and roll onto one side, to slowly come out of it.

If you carry a lot of tension in your jaw or grind your teeth at night, you may want to spend some time practicing hip-opening postures. A very supportive, relaxing hip opening posture is **reclined butterfly pose**. Lie on your back with your arms resting out to your side, palms facing up towards the ceiling. Bring the soles of your feet together with the sides of the feet touching the ground. The knees are relaxed out to the sides of the body. For more knee support, place pillows underneath them. Stay here for several minutes, concentrating on a relaxing, slow breath. Also concentrate on relaxing the muscles of your face and jaw. When you are ready to release the posture, slowly extend your feet out to straighten your legs.

While you are in bed, you can practice the **counting meditation**. Come into a position lying on your back and connect with your **full yogic breath**. Begin to count down from 9 to 1, taking in a breath and breathing it out for each number. If you lose track of what number you are on, start back again at 9. Continue this until you drift off to sleep.... ♟

CHAPTER 10

Developing Your Own Practice Routine

As you can see, there are many exercises, breathing routines, meditations, and visualizations. It is important to be able to develop your own practice routines and allow yourself the freedom to vary and change these routines, as you need. How many times have you set out to do a certain exercise routine only to fail because you can't reach your goal? It is important to be realistic and also to be flexible. Sometimes, we need more of a physical workout, and sometimes we need more of a supportive and relaxing routine. With all of the various exercises we have learned, you can develop routines to fit your particular needs.

We have already learned several ways to incorporate breath, meditation, visualization, and alignment into our musical practice. We will now explore ways to develop a yoga routine to help strengthen, stretch, rejuvenate, and relax our being.

Developing a routine can be difficult, especially since many of us already feel that our lives are filled to the maximum. If we set smaller goals, it can be more gratifying and easier to attain our goals. You may also want to connect your yoga practice to another activity that you do every day. For example, you have to wake up and go to sleep every day. You may want to practice early in the morning before you do anything else, or practice before you go to bed to relax the body and mind.

Start all of your practice routines with a brief centering meditation to bring all of your attention to the present moment and to release the mind from your other activities. Bring your attention to your breath. When the breath is firmly established, then come into your warm-ups and poses. Remember to take several deep breaths into each one of your stretches and postures. Pause periodically throughout your practice, and notice any sensations in the body. Also, pause between sides to notice the difference between each side.

PRACTICE ROUTINES

Throughout this book, I have listed various routines to get you started on your daily practice. I encourage you to practice the various poses presented, then see which ones work well for you and create your own routine depending on how much time you have. If you only have a few minutes, connect with your breath. Stretch and move in any way that feels good for you. Notice your posture throughout the day, such as while you are standing in line, while you are seated at a desk, and while you are playing your instrument. Practice elongating the spine, lifting through the crown of your head, and relaxing the shoulders back and down in everything you do. Practice being mindful as you go about your daily activities. Bring awareness to your breath throughout the day, and practice lengthening the breath.

In the following pages, I have included all of the charts from each chapter so that you can use them as a menu from which to choose a variety of breaths, meditations, and postures. In the charts, I have listed some of the benefits for each technique or posture and also their page numbers for easy reference. You can use these charts to create your own practice routines to suit your specific needs. I suggest having a varied routine that will get you through the week. Cover all of the different aspects of making the mind-body connection, helping yourself with your performance schedule and enhancing your daily life.

To get the full benefit from practicing yoga, you should have a regular routine that you can do each day. It can be anywhere from 10 to 30 minutes or more, depending on your schedule. Some days, you may have more time, so you can lengthen your routine. Other days, you may only have 10 minutes. The length of your practice doesn't matter, but the regularity of your practice is important.

Breathing Techniques

Breath	Benefits	Page
Full Yogic Breath (Three Part *Dirgha* Breath)	basic breath for developing awareness	12
Ocean Breath (*Ujjayi*)	brings focus and concentration on the breath; calms, relaxes, and centers us	15
Alternate Nostril Breathing (*Nadi Shodhana*)	very calming and relaxing	16
Conductor Breath	very energizing and uplifting	17
Helicopter Breath	very energizing and balancing	18

Meditation Techniques

Meditations	Benefits	Page
Breath	relaxes the mind	25
Mantra	promotes peace	28
Counting	releases the mind fully	29
Walking Meditation	calms the entire being	31
Meditation in Motion	brings meditation to daily activities	32
Visualization Meditations	helps prepare for specific events	36

Upper Body Exercises

Exercise	Benefits	Page
Fingers	important to keep limber for performance	55
Lion Pose	stretches and relaxes face muscles	56
Hands	helps prevent overuse injuries	56
Wrist and Arm Rotations	essential for flexibility	57
Shoulders: Tension and Release	exaggerates the tension, then lets it go to feel relaxed	57
Shoulder Circles	releases tension in the shoulders and upper back	57
Neck Circles	releases tension in the neck	58
Shoulder Stretch	opens the space between the shoulder blades	59
Tricep Stretch	stretches the under part of the arm	59
Cow Face Arms	stretches the triceps, shoulders, and chest	60
Eagle Arms	stretches the shoulders and upper back	60
Standing Yoga Mudra	opens the chest and shoulders; stretches the legs	61
Helicopter	energizes and releases tension in the body	63

Spine Exercises

Exercise	Benefits	Page
Table Pose	elongates the spine	69
Cat and Dog Stretch	opens front and back of the body	71
Back Strengthener	strengthens the entire back	72
Opening the Sides of the Body	expands rib cage for breath	72
Thread the Needle	stretches the shoulders, upper back, arms, and neck	73
Forward Bend	lengthens the entire back of the body	74
Extended Child Pose	stretches the spine and relaxes the nervous system	75
Spinal Twist	spinal alignment	76
Staff Pose	strengthens hamstrings and back; improves posture	77
Staff Pose with Arms Extended	strengthens the entire back of the body	79
Water Wheels	strengthens abdominal muscles	80

Lower Body Exercises

Exercise	Benefits	Page
Warrior 1	helps to stand your ground; strengthens legs, hips, and shoulders	83
Warrior 2	helps to open hips, chest, and shoulders	84
Side Angle Warrior	opens hips, shoulders, and the entire side of the body	85
Reversed Warrior	opens up rib cage, strengthens lower body	86
Triangle	strengthens core of the body, legs, hips and shoulders	87

Balance, Focus, and Concentration Exercises

Exercise	Benefits	Page
Balancing Pose	warm-up, prepares mind and body for balancing exercises	92
Tree	opens hips; strengthens legs; lengthens spine	93
Warrior 3	lengthens entire body; strengthens legs, shoulders, and back	94
Eagle Pose	stretches hips, upper back, and shoulders; strengthens legs	96

When you develop your own practice routine, make sure that it includes the following sections listed in the "Practice Routine Chart" on the following page. Choose whatever exercise you would like to do for a particular day. If you would like to work on a particular section more, then do more exercises in that area. You can vary the order of the sections, but you should always start with a brief centering exercise to focus the mind on the present moment. Bring your attention to the **full yogic breath**, and relax the muscles in the body. You can also create an intention for your practice on that particular day. It is important to rest in *shavasana* for about 5 minutes at the end of each session to allow the body and mind to relax and integrate the various postures.

Use the chart on page 114 below to fill in your own particular routines. I have listed sample routines that you can try for the week. Sometimes, you will need more of a relaxing routine. Other days, you will need more of an energetic routine.

I have listed various sample routines for a week according to what you would like to receive energetically. Practice these routines anywhere from 10 to 20 minutes. If you have 30 minutes or more, you can pick a specific category and do more exercises for that area. Choose another area of the body to focus on the next time you practice.

Practice Routines

Divide Your Practice Routines into These Parts:	Choose Exercises That You Would Like to Do Each Day from Each Category
Breath	
Meditation	
Upper Body	
Spine	
Lower Body	
Balance	
Relaxation	

DAY 1   Practice Routine

Divide Your Practice Routines into These Parts:	Relaxing Routine	Page
Breath	Alternate Nostril	16
Meditation	Counting: make the exhales longer than inhales	29
Upper Body	Neck Circles, Shoulder Circles	57
Spine	Forward Bend, Spinal Twists	74, 76
Lower Body	Warrior 1	83
Balance	Tree	93
Relaxation	Shavasana	105

DAY 2   Practice Routine

Divide Your Practice Routines into These Parts:	Invigorating Routine	Page
Breath	Conductor	17
Meditation	Meditation in Motion – make your entire routine a meditation	32
Upper Body	Shoulders: Tension and Release, Yoga Mudra	57
Spine	Forward Bend, Spinal Twists	74, 76
Lower Body	Warrior 2, Side Angle Warrior	84, 85
Balance	Warrior 3	94
Relaxation	Shavasana	105

DAY 3   Practice Routine

Divide Your Practice Routines into These Parts:	Developing Focus and Concentration Routine	Page
Breath	Ocean Breath	15
Meditation	Mantra	28
Upper Body	Wrist and Arm Rotations, Cow Face Arms	56, 59
Spine	Spinal Twist	76
Lower Body	Warrior 2, Reversed Warrior	84, 86
Balance	Eagle Pose	96
Relaxation	Shavasana	105

DAY 4   Practice Routine

Divide Your Practice Routines into These Parts:	Strengthening Routine	Page
Breath	Ocean Breath	15
Meditation	Visualization: visualize yourself being strong in body, mind, and spirit	36
Upper Body	Standing Yoga Mudra	60
Spine	Back Strengthener, Staff Pose	72, 77
Lower Body	Triangle	87
Balance	Warrior 3 Arm Variations	95
Relaxation	Shavasana	105

DAY 5 Practice Routine

Divide Your Practice Routines into These Parts:	Developing Flexibility Routine	Page
Breath	Full Yogic Breath	12
Meditation	Breath	25
Upper Body	Wrist and Arm Rotations, Shoulder and Neck Circles	57, 58
Spine	Cat and Dog Stretch, Open Sides of the Body, Forward Bend	71, 72, 74
Lower Body	Side Angle Warrior	85
Balance	Tree	93
Relaxation	Shavasana	105

DAY 6 Practice Routine

Divide Your Practice Routines into These Parts:	Balancing Routine	Page
Breath	Alternate Nostril Breathing	16
Meditation	Counting: focus on counting the same number for both the inhalation and exhalation	29
Upper Body	Helicopter	62
Spine	Cat and Dog Stretch, Extended Child Pose	71, 72, 75
Lower Body	Reversed Warrior	86
Balance	Eagle Pose	96
Relaxation	Shavasana	105

DAY 7 Day of Rest

If you have more time, concentrate on different areas of the body for a particular day. Add these sequences to your routine above, but give more time to these specific areas.

10 Minute Upper Body Routine	10 Minute Spine Routine	10 Minute Lower Body Routine	10 Minute Balance Routine
Neck and Shoulder Circles	Cat and Dog Stretch	Warrior 1	Mountain Pose: connect with breath and focal point
Finger Stretches	Opening the Sides of the Body	Warrior 2	Balancing Pose Warm-Up
Wrist and Arm Rotations	Back Strengthener	Side Angle Warrior	Tree Pose
Standing Yoga Mudra	Thread the Needle	Reversed Warrior	Eagle Pose
Eagle Arms	Staff Pose	Triangle	Helicopter Breath
Helicopter	Staff Pose with Arms Extended	Conductor Breath	Mountain Pose: notice how you feel

Yoga and Awareness "Off the Mat"

Yoga "off the mat" refers to how we bring the yoga concepts into our daily lives. This is what we have been doing throughout this book, applying yoga to our musical activities. As we begin to practice meditation, breath awareness, stretches, and poses, we can make more of a mind–body connection in all that we do. We start to realize that we can shape our world by how we think and act. My motto is, "Yoga off the mat is where it's at."

Why do we practice all of these exercises and meditations in the first place? We practice to help us in our daily lives and in making music. Yoga really becomes a life practice and a way of life. If you can take these concepts into your daily life, this will help you make more informed choices and help you enjoy your music making more. This is a long-term process, which varies differently upon personal needs and practice.

The tools we learn in yoga, such as awareness of the body, mind, posture, and breath, can bring awareness to the choices we make every day. For example, if you keep playing your instrument and your body is hurting, you should probably change something so that it does not hurt. You learn that maybe you need to change the way you hold your instrument, or that maybe you need to stretch before you practice, or take little breaks every so often when you are practicing. You will also notice other choices that you make in life and the cause and effect of these choices, such as if you eat this particular food, how would you feel? If you keep telling yourself that you cannot do a certain thing, will you ever be able to do it? What is the mind chatter telling you time after time? It becomes a daily practice of being mindful of the choices we make and to have compassion with ourselves if we get off track. We learn to let go of the mind chatter and stay centered.

We all have different kinds of habits. Some are good for us and lead us closer to our goal. Some are not so good for us and take us further away from our goal. Practicing mindfulness in all that we do can lead us closer to our goal. We take responsibility for our choices.

Taking yoga classes is a great way to learn new postures and new techniques. It can challenge you in ways that you may not challenge yourself. When you practice a particular pose that is challenging for you, and your mind says, "I don't like this pose," or "I can't do this pose," step back from the mind chatter and notice how you treat those challenges. If you can bring more awareness to how you practice "on the mat," your mind will most likely respond the same way in your daily challenges "off the mat."

When we practice yoga, we are really practicing a way of life. We bring more awareness to our daily practice and choices. We become aware of breath and posture and how they relate to the body and the mind. When we practice a particular pose and notice all of the thoughts that come during our practice and how we deal with those thoughts, that sheds light on how we usually think when we are doing our daily tasks. You can learn to observe your mind chatter at a distance, detaching yourself. You will find that your true center is separate from your thoughts. You will learn to have more compassion for yourself, keeping the judges at bay.

Earlier, I mentioned the student who was concerned that he was developing such an awareness of everything in his life that it was overwhelming. If this happens, it is important to have compassion. Awareness is great, as it can help you make more informed choices, but if you become aware of habits that you want to change, take it one step at a time. Don't feel that you have to change everything all at once. You will need to accept where you are at this point in time and be okay with it. Always practice your music and yoga with patience and compassion.

Watch your mind and thoughts, find your edge, and breathe into that edge. When we become the witness, we observe our thoughts and do not judge them. By practicing being the witness, we come to realize that we are not our thoughts. In between each of these thoughts, we begin to observe a brief stillness or calmness. When we practice meditation, we will see this space in between the thoughts get a little bigger. This space of silence and calmness is our center. We practice to get in touch with our center so that no matter what arises in our life, we realize that we have this stillness, this calm center with us and in us all of the time, no matter where we go or what we do.

Witness and observe without judgment. Our minds always want to label everything, because it is easier for us to put it into a particular compartment. Can you observe without labels? Just watch and observe all of those thoughts with no judgment. This is the witness.

We don't always have to have a particular routine to practice, but doing so can make "yoga off the mat" easier. If we have practiced getting in touch with our center, developing focus and concentration, meditating, and releasing the mind chatter, we will gain more confidence so that when challenges come, we will stay centered and will be able to handle the situation with much more grace and ease. The more we learn how we treat ourselves and what our thoughts are as we practice challenging poses, the more we can learn to observe our thoughts and actions when challenges come into our lives.

As stated earlier, sometimes the postures and stretches we dislike are the ones that we need the most. If this happens on the mat, it is sure to happen in our daily lives. What might you be avoiding in your daily life because you know it would be uncomfortable to deal with? Practicing yoga can give us the strength and encouragement to accept life's challenges no matter how hard they may be.

When we practice being the observer, we learn to develop peace and compassion. We don't attach ourselves to these thoughts or feelings. When we practice yoga, we practice becoming present in all that we do, and we practice how to release judgment. The idea is that we carry this knowledge that we gain when we are on the mat into our daily lives. We bring consciousness and awareness to the choices that we make and the actions that we do.

May your practice and performances be filled with inspiration and awareness.

Namaste.

Resources

WEB SITES

www.yogajournal.com
www.abc-of-yoga.com
www.miamarieolson.com
www.artistshousemusic.com

READING

Austin, Miriam. *Meditation for Wimps: Finding Your Balance in an Imperfect World.* New York: Sterling Publishing Co., Inc., 2003.

Benson, Herbert, M.D., with Miriam Z. Klipper. *The Relaxation Response.* New York: Harpertorch, 2000.

Borysenko, Joan, Ph.D., with Larry Rothstein. *Minding the Body, Mending the Mind.* New York: Bantam New Age Books, 1988.

Dass, Ram. *Journey of Awakening: A Meditator's Guidebook.* Rev. ed. Edited by Daniel Goleman with Dwarkanath Bonner and Ram Dev (Dale Borglum). New York: Bantam Books, 1990.

Faulds, Richard, and Senior Teachers of Kripalu Center for Yoga and Health. *Kripalu Yoga: A Guide to Practice On and Off the Mat.* New York: Bantam Dell, 2005.

Green, Barry, and W. Timothy Gallwey. *The Inner Game of Music.* New York: Anchor Press/Doubleday, 1986.

Judith, Anodea, Ph.D. *Wheels of Life: A User's Guide to the Chakra System.* 2nd ed. St. Paul: Llewellyn Publications, 2003.

Khalsa, Shakta Kaur. *Kundalini Yoga: Unlock Your Inner Potential through Life-Changing Exercise.* Project Editors Barbara M. Berger and Crystal A. Coble. New York: Dorling Kindersley Publishing Inc., 2001.

Miller, Olivia H. *The Yoga Deck.* Yoga Consultant: Katherine
  Trainor. San Francisco: Chronicle Books, 2001. Deck of cards.

Ristad, Eloise. *A Soprano on Her Head.* Utah: Real People Press, 1982.

Sivananda Yoga Vedanta Centre. *101 Essential Tips: Yoga.* Editors
  Lucinda Hawksley, Ian Whitelaw. London: Dorling Kindersley
  Publishing, Inc., 1995.

Tolle, Ekhart. *The Power of Now: A Guide to Spiritual Enlighten-
  ment.* New World Library, 1999.

Werner, Kenny. *Effortless Mastery.* Indiana: Jamey Aebersol Jazz,
  Inc., 1996.

About the Author

Photo by Mia Olson

I started taking piano lessons when I was eight years old, and a couple of years later started playing the flute. Practicing was always fun for me, especially the flute, and I practiced all of the time. Flute became my primary instrument and I ended up pursuing a degree in classical flute performance at the Univiersity of Wisconsin-Madison. From there, I went on to earn a degree in jazz flute performance at Berklee College of Music in Boston and a Master's degree in contemporary improvisation at New England Conservatory of Music.

Throughout these years of playing every day, I found a need to exercise and stretch as most musicians need to do after extended periods of playing. Yoga seemed to suit this specific need, and I realized it offered so much more than any other form of exercise. Through practicing yoga, I became more aware of my posture and noticed that this shift in awareness helped me stand taller, which also affected my outlook and mental state. Practicing yoga helped me to feel more grounded and stronger, yet centered and peaceful at the same time.

I was feeling much better physically and mentally. I noticed that I was able to focus much more when I was practicing my instrument and doing other tasks. I also felt more of a connection to spirit; I felt an inner peace. As I played my instrument, I became much more physically aware of how I was holding my posture and my instrument and started to make shifts so that I could play with ease. I started using simple breath awareness and visualization before a performance so that I could play my best, calm my nerves and stay present. Practicing yoga really changed my outlook on the world.

With all of these benefits and positive changes, I was craving to learn more. I started looking into where I could receive yoga training. Most of the teachers I studied with received their yoga certification from Kripalu, in western Massachusetts. I researched various places, and understood why they chose Kripalu. I wanted a place to learn that was not into the guru mentality. I decided to go out for a few days on a rest and relaxation retreat to check it out. I fell in love with the place and its philosophy.

After my initial experience at Kripalu, I applied for the teacher-training program there. My experience with yoga was helping and changing me in so many ways that I thought that it was really powerful, and I wanted to learn more. Not only did I want to learn more to help myself, but I also wanted to be able to share this knowledge with the Berklee community. At this time I was the assistant chair of the harmony department at Berklee, doing more administrative work than teaching. I received my 200-hour basic certification from Kripalu. After I was done, I started teaching a weekly course for faculty and staff, gearing it towards stress reduction. The class really responded to this physical and mental release. I also wanted to share this knowledge with Berklee students, so I developed a *Musician's Yoga* course.

Shortly after my certification, I became the acting chair of my department and was getting deeper into administration. I started teaching a *Musician's Yoga* class that was populated within hours of its posting. I was asked if I could open up another section, which I did, and this was also filled immediately. The students were craving this connection with mind and body. I was feeling a call to work more with the students in this yoga for musicians area, so I made the choice of going back to the faculty. It has proven to be one of the best decisions that I have ever made. I have a nice blend of teaching music and yoga. I feel that I can best help the students by sharing this knowledge so that they may use these skills to help themselves in their lives as musicians, and their lives in general.

Since my initial certification in yoga, I went on to get my Professional Level, 500-hour Kripalu Yoga teacher training certification. In addition to teaching these classes at Berklee, I have been teaching *Musician's Yoga* seminars for various music organizations and music festivals around the world. While sharing my experiences and knowledge with other musicians, I have found that so many musicians are starving for this knowledge. I was driven to write this book as a request from so many people around me and to share with more musicians throughout the world.

INDEX